PATHS OF FIRE

PATHS OF FIRE

THE GUN AND THE WORLD IT MADE

ANDREW NAHUM

REAKTION BOOKS
Published in association with
the Science Museum, London

TO FIONA, ADAM AND CHLOE

Published by Reaktion Books Ltd
Unit 32, Waterside
44–48 Wharf Road
London N1 7UX, UK
www.reaktionbooks.co.uk

In association with the Science Museum
Exhibition Road
London SW7 2DD, UK
www.sciencemuseum.org.uk

First published 2021

Printed and bound in Great Britain
by TJ Books Ltd, Padstow, Cornwall

A catalogue record for this book is available from the British Library

ISBN: 978 1 78914 397 3

CONTENTS

A 90 mm M1 anti-aircraft
gun on display to the
public at Watertown
Arsenal, Massachusetts,
c. 1950.

PREFACE

Type 'Mikhail Kalashnikov' into an Internet search engine like Google and the biography of the inventor comes back to you from secretive server sites in Oregon or Virginia in a blink, winging down optical fibres at the speed of light, or even along some old-style electrical phone cable, but still covering almost 200,000 km an hour (124,000 mph).

Squeeze the trigger of a Kalashnikov, and a bullet weighing about a quarter of an ounce is kicked up the barrel at a trivial fraction of that speed, propelled by a chemical bang that would have been quite familiar to Oliver Cromwell or General Custer. Modernity, in the everyday sense, is not evenly distributed. Ancient inventions, like the gun, are often still as prevalent, and as effective in their own domains, as those embodying the latest science.

Antique, yet contemporary, the gun dominates the world in obvious ways and is woven into the fabric of life, even though people in fortunate countries do not see them very often. But the influence of guns extends even beyond war, revolution and death, and this is not a conventional book about them. Nor is it about the gun lobby or the profound effects that firearms have on national affairs and on civil society.

Neither is it a synoptic history. There is no seamless arc, for example, from muskets to Kalashnikovs, or from the Renaissance cannon to the immense naval guns that could strike from 16 km (10 mi.) at Jutland – although these things are all here.

Rather, this is a series of snapshots, showing how guns and gunnery have influenced our world and our culture in unsuspected, surprising ways. The flight of the cannon ball, for instance, helped overturn ancient theories of motion, inherited from the Greeks and clung to by the Catholic Church, for it was the study of ballistics, as well as the study of the heavens, that helped underpin the new science of Galileo and Newton. In spite of theology, here was an analysis that was seen to be genuinely useful by the most powerful actors in the emerging scientific world.

In the Second World War, predicting and calculating the aim of anti-aircraft batteries required the creation of small reactive 'on board' computers, a development which points to a different history of computing and not the familiar one based on vast static mainframe machines. It is an alternative story because these new devices opened the path to artificial intelligence, to robotics, and even to the way in which we make sense of our own consciousness and powers of action today.

In another sphere, gun making refined the techniques and set the style for modern manufacture – the systems that now produce so much *stuff* for us, so accurately and so cheaply.

Firearms – and not just battles – have also moulded political and international structures in intricate and surprising ways. Ronald Reagan's Star Wars programme precipitated the end of the Cold War and also, perhaps, the end of the apparently impermeable Soviet empire. But at the heart of Reagan's sally was an ultimately idealized gun – Edward Teller's X-ray laser – which existed only as a mythic weapon, an unrealized design that will, perhaps, never be made. Yet this promised ray gun proved to be an immensely effective lever during the years of the Reagan–Gorbachev diplomacy and provoked a seismic geopolitical shift. Its power was that it seemed to promise a 'nuclear umbrella', a robust new American defence against incoming missiles that would end the balance of nuclear terror.

It is a truism that arms development has an enormous and continuing effect on technological development and on social change. But the histories here show that this effect occurs not just in the familiar ways we know, but often by elliptical and surprising routes. The events here reflect these unexpected linkages. These are the less-considered tributaries of arms development, which also link to the broader, more generous and more surprising history of technology that has begun to emerge in recent years. These are episodes crammed with lesser known cross-connections, with individuals, and with contingencies that reveal an unsuspected undertow to the conventional and established tide of historical events.

Newton as 'Olympian'. The original 1731 design for Isaac Newton's memorial in Westminster Abbey by William Kent. For some reason Pope's couplet was not used, and there is a much longer Latin inscription.

THE GEOMETRY OF WAR

In 1931 a high-powered Soviet delegation attended the International Congress of the History of Science and Technology, held that year at the Science Museum in London. The members even arrived by aeroplane, then an emphatic statement of importance, and it has become a notable event for the history of science. It was, one historian commented, a 'Soviet road show' since, instead of just the one speaker the conference expected, 'a small battalion' (actually eight delegates) arrived, led by Nikolai Bukharin, once a close associate of Lenin. It was impossible to fit in papers from all the delegates but they were mollified by being given time for two papers and the publication of all the contributions at lightning speed – an editorial marathon 'Five Day Plan' based at the Soviet Embassy that resulted in the influential small volume *Science at the Crossroads*.[1]

By far the most influential contribution to both the spoken session and the book, however, came from a comparatively little-known Soviet philosopher and physicist, Boris Hessen, with his paper 'The Social and Economic Roots of Newton's Principia', which located Newton's 'pure' science firmly in the social milieu of its times and even in contemporary industrial and military events.[2]

The paper, according to one reading, was written 'with an eye to saving [Hessen's] career (and possibly his neck)', since it was delivered in the presence of Ernst Kolman, 'arguably the most savage of Stalin's intellectual cheerleaders', the delegate who had been assigned to the group by the Politburo and charged with reporting on the political behaviour of the ideologically suspect members Bukharin and Hessen.[3]

Hessen's talk, the most startling and influential of the session, was an explicit attack on the notion of pure science and on the role of personal genius, taking Isaac Newton as the case study, asking 'where is the source of Newton's genius? . . . What determined the content and direction of his work?' And he teed up his analysis by quoting, parodically, Alexander Pope's epitaph: 'Nature and Nature's laws lay hid in night: God said, Let Newton be! and all was light.'[4]

Hessen announced that he would apply dialectical materialism and Marx's conception of the historical process to the phenomenon of Newton's work. In British scientific tradition, and even within the then relatively immature study of the history of science, it was conventional, certainly, to assign the phenomenon of Newton and his work to the 'benevolence of divine providence', or at least to a rare and exceptional chance that brought forth his personal genius. Simon Schaffer, in his paper 'Newton at the Crossroads', has pointed out that here Hessen is drawing on arguments from Engels, as in his 1894 letter insisting that

> science depends far more on the state . . . and the requirements of technique . . . If society has a technical need, that helps science forward more than ten universities. The whole of hydrostatics (Torricelli etc.) was called forth by the necessity for regulating mountain streams of Italy in the 16th and 17th centuries . . . But unfortunately, it has become the custom to write the history of the sciences as if they had fallen from the skies.[5]

But in Hessen's materialist reading, economic circumstances and the methods of production condition the 'social, political and intellectual life processes of society'. 'The ideas of the ruling class are, in every historical age, the ruling ideas'. Furthermore, 'the ruling class subjects . . . all other classes to its interests,' and Hessen rattled off a list of practical problems of the day including canal-building, ship stability, mechanical hoists and pulleys for mines, cogwheels and transmission mechanisms for mills, and a host of techno-scientific problems.

Newton's physics, therefore, was based on the ideology of the ruling class in the seventeenth century and the emergent English bourgeoisie. The period at which Newton was at the peak of his activity, noted Hessen, coincided with the English Civil War and the Commonwealth and so he set out a brief history of ballistics, essentially the problem of aiming cannon at a distance and the influence of various scientists on the art.

Furthermore, the rising mercantile and manufacturing bourgeoisie brought 'natural science into its service, into the service of the developing productive forces' and, as further evidence of Newton's practicality and the instrumental service he, in effect, provided to these classes, Hessen quoted Newton's letter to his friend Francis Aston, who had asked for advice on what he should investigate on his European tour in order 'to utilise his journey most rationally'.[6]

Newton had a long list. Aston should study methods of steering and navigating ships, carefully survey 'all the fortresses he should happen upon, their method of construction, their poweres of resistance', study methods of obtaining metals from ores, find out if it was true that 'in Hungary, Slovakia and Bohemia, near the town of Eila . . . there were rivers whose waters contained gold,' to find out how the Dutch protected their vessels from worm and whether clocks were any use in determining longitude. He must visit a newly established glass-polishing factory in Holland (presumably for lenses). He also added a considerable section on investigating whether the art of transmuting one metal into another existed in those places.

Newton had also, Hessen reminds us, brought improvements to stamping or casting coins during his term as Master of the Royal Mint from 1699 to 1727 and showed a sophisticated interest in the exchange rates of gold and silver in various countries. Hessen wrote:

We cite all these facts as a counterweight to the traditional representation of Newton . . . as an 'Olympian' standing high above all 'terrestrial' technical and economic interests of his time and soaring only in the lofty realms of abstract thought . . . We have come to the end of our analysis of the Principia. We have shown how its physical content arose out of the tasks of that era, which were placed on the agenda by the class that was coming to power.[7]

The talk was greeted with enormous enthusiasm by politically active scientists including the Marxist crystallographer J. D. Bernal, the bio-chemist (and Sinologist) Joseph Needham and the science writer J. G. Crowther.

For Bernal, concerned to emphasize both the social relevance of science and the social framework from which it sprang, the paper was genuinely revelatory: Hessen had provided the framework.[8] Indeed, it 'turned out to be the most influential paper presented at the conference. In Britain it brought together under a common purpose an entire generation of left-leaning scientific celebrities from John Haldane to John Bernal. Internationally, it inspired an approach to the history of science which still holds sway today.'[9]

'THE FRINGES OF SCIENCE'

The issues cited by Hessen were indeed powerful influences on the science of their day, although their role in relation to Isaac Newton is more complex than Hessen, perhaps, allowed.

Moreover, gunnery was to prove remarkably influential, not just by affecting the way scientific history came to be seen and written in the twentieth century (which is, after all, a meta-study) but perhaps more intriguingly to the actual construction of the new science of the sixteenth and seventeenth centuries. Many of Newton's contemporaries and predecessors were deeply influenced by the emerging problems of ballistics and how to predict range and deliver accurate fire. These problems created, arguably, a revolution in thought that helped to propel early modern science and demolished the ancient theories of motion that had been inherited from Aristotle.

Theories of motion in the sixteenth century seem now confusing and paradoxical. Aristotle had held that bodies naturally tend to a state of rest. Birds flew because their feathers had a light, airy affinity to the sky. Smoke rose, perhaps to the Moon. Stones and cannon balls fell to their natural resting place because they had a base, earthy tendency. There was no concept of momentum (but why did a pendulum work: should it not stop at the bottom of its arc?). Things moved because they were given a push that eventually ran out, although in time Newton was to prove something quite contrary – that bodies continue in a uniform state of motion (or rest) until acted on by an external force. But for complex reasons, and after much contention, Aristotle's theories of motion and of matter had become part of Catholic thinking.

But, like the Large Hadron Collider today, the cannon could do violent things to matter and elicit phenomena that had never been seen before. Before the cannon, man-made objects had never been projected so far, and with such force and speed. Ballistics provided a lever to pry open this synthesis of classical and medieval doctrine.

Nevertheless, to more traditional and less ideologically inclined historians like George Clark, who was at Oxford in the 1930s, the idea that the great inferences of physics had been derived by scientists dancing to the tune of soldiers, merchants and manufacturers seemed entirely misguided. Although Clark did acknowledge the effects of war, religion and medicine, he vigorously defended the notion of the idealized academic life, 'the disinterested desire to know, the impulse of the mind to exercise itself methodically and without any practical purpose'. Indeed, for Clark, it was the social function of universities 'to set free . . . men who had the desire to know from the pressure of other motives'.[10]

Another young historian, A. Rupert Hall, this time at Cambridge, decided to tackle the subject of ballistics.[11] He set out, in part, to show that the emerging scientific theory on ballistics had been irrelevant to gunnery. Early science, he contended, failed to influence military technology because 'the gun in itself was so inconsistent in its behaviour that great accuracy . . . in laying the gun . . . was labour in vain. Nothing was uniform . . . powder varied in strength by as much as twenty percent; shot differed widely in weight, diameter, density and degree of roundness.'[12]

Cannon and shot also had a large allowance for 'windage', the difference in diameter between the ball and the barrel, since out-of-round or misshapen shot might otherwise jam on firing with disastrous consequences. Therefore the ball took an 'ambiguous bouncing path' along the barrel of the gun and there was no confidence that 'the line of sight would be the line of flight'. In gunnery trials in the 1730s it was shown that shots could be as much as 100 yards left or right of the mark, and though one shot might reach it, the next could fall short by as much as 200 yards. Hall noted the astronomer and scientist Edmond Halley's observation that gunners 'loose all the geometrical accuracy of their art from ye unfitness of ye ball to ye bore and ye uncertain reverse [recoil] of ye gun which is indeed very hard to overcome'.[13]

Hall also wanted to contest Hessen's analysis of Newton, suggesting that

> when Hessen wrote that the scheme of seventeenth century physics 'was mainly determined by the economic and social tasks which the rising bourgeoisie raised to the forefront' he was guilty of a gross anachronism since the level of physics which Newton approaches in the *Principia* was only reached by an original intellectual process, not directly from the empirical industry of his day.[14]

But this was a problematic argument since Hall surely knew that earlier philosophers had often been eager to emphasize the utility of their science and the link between military engineering and emergent science was clear. Early modern scientists, and Galileo in particular, explicitly put their learning at the service of their rulers. Galileo wrote treatises on military engineering for the Medici family and had been a tutor on scientific matters to the future Grand Duke of Tuscany, Cosimo II. Indeed, the first systematic book on gunnery, *Nova scientia*, published in Venice in 1537 by Niccolò Fontana Tartaglia, a mathematics teacher, was dedicated to Francesco Maria I della Rovere, Duke of Urbino,

Supreme General of the Venetian army and leader of a military coalition against the Ottoman empire. Tartaglia claimed to have devised mathematical rules for setting the range of the cannon according to its elevation. The book has possibly the first illustration showing the use of the *squadra*, or gunner's quadrant, for setting the elevation of the piece.

Nevertheless, Tartaglia's attempt to define the trajectory (the path of the projectile) was based on Aristotelian theory. This gave a trajectory with three components: a violent initial straight climb from the gun, a mixed motion, shown as the arc of a true circle, as the violent motion faded, and finally a direct, vertical fall to earth.[15]

One application of his theory concerned a problem posed by the Duke of Urbino regarding the effect of cannon at different heights and distances. Tartaglia believed that the lower, more distant cannon would

Portrait of Niccolò Tartaglia from the title page of his work, *Quesiti et inventioni diverse* (1554).

The gunner's quadrant or *squadra* as illustrated in Niccolò Tartaglia's *La nova scientia* (1537). The weighted bob is free to hang down vertically, with the scale showing the elevation of the barrel above the horizontal.

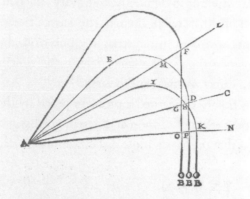

Tartaglia's idealized trajectory from *La nova scientia* (1537). The first part of the trajectory is straight, because it is the result of an Aristotelian violent, unnatural force, while the next intermediate part is an arc of a circle until finally the projectile descends vertically under the influence of natural motion. This misleading theory was promulgated by other writers for at least 150 years, long after Galileo had shown that the true path was parabolic.

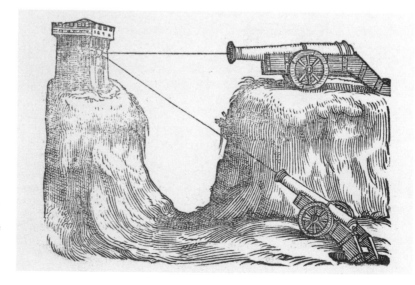

Tartaglia's analysis of the efficacy of cannon fire at different heights and distances in response to a problem posed by the Duke of Urbino, Supreme General of the Venetian army. Tartaglia believed, incorrectly, that the lower cannon would do more damage because the elevation preserved the violent portion of the trajectory.

do more damage because the higher firing angle or elevation would preserve the violent portion of the trajectory for longer.

He also claimed that just one trial shot from a cannon could be used to calculate its calibration and allow it to be set to fire accurately out to every distance within its capacity. Hall and subsequent writers, however, have suggested that Tartaglia's secret notes for gunners, what now would be called 'firing tables', which relate the target distance to the elevation of the piece and the size of charge and ball, were not mathematical but empirical and practical. They derived from actual gunnery experience and had been gleaned by Tartaglia from experienced cannoneers. The mathematics, Hall implied, was merely a gloss to claim authority and influence, curry favour with patrons and win patronage.

Hall dealt roughly with Niccolò Tartaglia and almost all the early writers on gunnery with their 'half intelligent, half decorative formulae', citing various seventeenth-century handbooks, and concluded that 'these works on artillery with their thoroughly medieval scientific background seem absurd and contemptible. How can their trifling arithmetical artifices compare with the imposing theorems of Galileo or the calculus of Newton and Leibniz?'[16]

Another target was the translation and publication in 1683 by Sir Jonas Moore of 'a mediocre Italian work of instruction' with the erroneous description of a cannon ball as having an initial straight-line flight of violent motion, then a curved section of 'mixt or crooked motion', and finally a vertical descent to the ground – a passage 'that would have said nothing new a hundred and fifty years before'.

Nevertheless, for Hall these misleading theories and textbooks 'were unimportant and had no effect on warlike operations so it was irrelevant whether or not a poor theory was replaced by a scientifically superior one'. What evidence, he challenged, 'is there that the rather pretentious theories of Tartaglia or Galileo were ever used as guides to the tactical employment of artillery?'

No calculation by gunners was necessary, Hall asserted, because in land war cannon were mostly placed as close as possible to the enemy ramparts, firing effectively at point-blank range to put repeated

Illustration from another late 17th-century gunnery treatise repeating the outmoded pre-Galilean ideas excoriated by A. Rupert Hall. From Samuel Sturmy, *The Mariner's Magazine; or, Sturmy's Mathematicall and Practicall Arts*, 1669, this edition, 1679, displayed in the 1996 exhibition, 'The Geometry of War', at the Museum of the History of Science in Oxford. Curators Jim Bennett and Stephen Johnston note that 'Just like Tartaglia almost 150 years earlier, he divided the path of artillery projectiles into three parts; an initial straight line of violent motion, then a curved section of "mixt or crooked motion" and finally the vertical descent to the ground of "natural motion".'

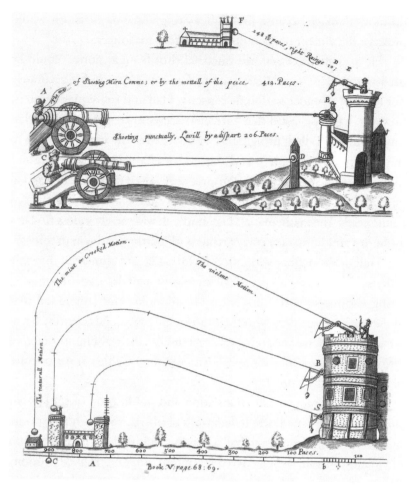

concentrated blows onto a small section of the fortifications and to open a breach. At sea 'nothing but point-blank fire was considered . . . to be worth the expense of powder.' Sir Walter Raleigh forbade his gunners to shoot at any greater range than point-blank.[17]

He conceded that 'in the sixteenth and seventeenth centuries the theory of projectiles offered the most useful and familiar approach' to these emerging scientific principles, and also admitted that the more subtle thinkers, 'philosophers from Galileo to Newton . . . used the problems of ballistics as a gymnasium in which to develop their powers for larger and more important researches.'

He asserted, however, that for the hapless gunners the claimed scientific basis of their art was spurious, perhaps until the accurately engineered artillery of the nineteenth century. Gunners were the 'first of all craftsmen to take up a cloak of science', but they 'struggled through many generations with one and another set of dogmas . . . in search of the mathematical formulae to rule their art, while always their tools remained undeveloped, incapable of using the worst of their theories'. Indeed, the poor gunner could hope for little more than to 'rise to be a workaday member of one of those groups which existed on the fringe of science, nourishing himself and his studies on the crumbs from philosophic feasts'.

Later writers have been far more generous to Tartaglia than was Hall, perhaps acknowledging the extraordinary difficulty of using and trying to extend a set of deeply established but misleading axioms which, moreover, had the authority of the Church. A more recent view is that Tartaglia's attempt to explain ballistics using Aristotelian physics was a necessary first step, for it 'subverted traditional conceptions of motion, creating a "fertile confusion" from which the new science was able to emerge'.[18]

What does seem clear is that mathematicians and enquirers found gunnery fascinating for, in effect, it furnished experiments that the natural philosopher could study and use to develop theory. Robert Boyle observed that

the Phenomena afforded us by these arts ought to be lookt upon as really belonging to the history of nature . . . and therefore . . . fall under the cognizance of the naturalist and challenge his spec-ulation . . . [and] contribute to the advancement of his knowledge, and consequently of his power.[19]

Since firearms produced violent effects on matter, making it behave in ways that human power could not emulate, and forced material objects into new relationships, gunpowder became, in effect, a 'philo-sophical substance'. A good example was Galileo's prediction that if a shot was fired vertically downwards onto a stone pavement from a hundred cubits (about 45 m or 150 ft) the lead shot would be less deformed than one fired from only a short distance due to the resistance of the air. The revived Aristotelian philosophy of the Renaissance held the opposite: the bullet from the higher point would be travelling faster since falling motion would be added to the violent speed of the shot. When this was actually tried, some twenty years after Galileo proposed it, his prediction was shown to be correct.[20]

Galileo's *Dialogue Concerning the Two Chief World Systems* (1632) frames the enquiry as a discourse between three participants, one of whom, Salviati (in effect the voice of Galileo), taunts the other disputant, Simplicio, with an insouciance he may have come to regret:

> I see you have hitherto been of that herd who, in order to learn how matters such as [motion] take place, and in order to acquire a knowledge of natural effects, do not betake themselves to ships, or crossbows, or cannons, but retire to their studies . . . to see whether Aristotle has said anything about them.

Although Galileo, with this work, seems to have disobeyed the injunction put on him by the Church some time earlier to maintain (and to believe) that Earth was the centre of the universe and not to promulgate Copernicanism, he seems to have hoped that by couching the discussion as a disputation and not as advocacy or as a treatise, he could avoid the ban. Some sources suggest that he had a licence from Pope Urban VIII to write the book, as long as it was framed as a discourse. However, in the following year he was put on trial.[21]

And so, it was the emerging theory of motion, and not just the arrangement of the heavens, that was on trial. Catherine Ann France, who has made an incisive study of these episodes, suggests that the Elizabethan mathematician, astronomer and gunner Thomas Digges may have been the first to suggest a link between motion on earth and motion in the heavens. This implied that 'it was impossible to deal with the trajectory of the cannon in isolation because it had become an essential cognitive step towards understanding motion universally.'[22]

In Italy Galileo realized that the flight of the cannon ball was not the product of the Aristotelian concepts of 'violent' and of 'natural' motion. Rather, it resulted from the interaction of the vertical and horizontal components of motion – 'the law of fall' (gravity) accelerating the ball downwards throughout its entire flight, and its horizontal motion, imparted to the ball by the cannon. This showed that the flight of the ball should now be seen as a parabola, and that (viewed from the side) the path of the ball was symmetrical about the highest point of its flight – a finding which defied Aristotle and falsified his laws of motion. His opponents also understood this connection, and so new theories of motion were, in themselves, contentious and ideologically dangerous since they could be linked to Copernicus and to an attack on the concept of the geocentric universe. Indeed, in the hands of Galileo's followers who worked on motion, 'the reality of the law of fall became a proxy for the argument for the reality of Copernicanism.'[23]

The danger of the accusation of heresy that these thinkers faced is implicit in the circumspect way that Jean Buridan, rather earlier, framed his own non-Aristotelian ideas of force and momentum:

> One could say . . . that God, when he created the Universe set each of the celestial spheres in motion as it pleased him, impressing on each of them an impetus which has moved it ever since. God has no longer to move these spheres . . . These impetūs which God impressed on the celestial bodies have not been reduced or destroyed by time . . . [as] there was no resistance which could corrupt and restrain these impetūs. All this I do not give as certain; I would merely ask theologians to teach me how all these things could come about.[24]

Aristotelian philosophy, as interpreted by Thomas Aquinus, helped to underpin much theological thinking. For example, Aristotle's theory of matter, in which objects were held to possess both 'substance' and 'accident', seemed to help explain the mystery of the Eucharist – the transformation of bread and wine in the Communion. Since Aristotelian theory was so deeply interwoven into theological thinking, tugging at any thread of it was dangerous. How much else might unravel?

Perhaps impelled by Bertolt Brecht's 1937 play *The Life of Galileo*, much study has been directed to Galileo and his trial. The events and the relationships are complex and contentious. One revisionist view even suggests that Galileo was unwise and overconfident – perhaps impertinent. But we also have the voice of a contemporary witness, John Milton, who addressed Parliament in 1644 to advocate freedom in publishing and noted:

> I would recount what I have seen and heard in other countries, where this kind of inquisition tyrannizes; when I have sat among the learned men, for that honour I had, and had been counted happy to be born in such a place of philosophic freedom, as they supposed England was, while they themselves did nothing but bemoan the servile condition into which learning amongst them was brought: that this was it which had damped the glory of Italian wits: that nothing had been written these many years but flattery and fustian. There it was that I found and visited the famous Galileo, grown old a prisoner to the Inquisition, for thinking in astronomy otherwise what the Franciscan and Dominican licencers thought.[25]

CANNONS IN WHITEHALL

Perhaps in contemporary England there was indeed more liberty. The meetings at Gresham College in London had nurtured ideas for a possible college 'for the Promotion of Physico-Mathematico-Experimental Learning', a project that matured in 1662 as the Royal Society, with King Charles II as patron, and with the ambition to try and understand all types of phenomena through observation and experiment, not through received doctrine.[26]

Among its early activities were trials by Lord Brouncker on 'the recoiling of guns'. The first were held in the court of Gresham College in the presence of members of the society, and the second took place in the Tiltyard at Whitehall. These tests were remarkably public and were widely observed. The spectators included Charles II and his brother James.

It seems likely that these 1661 firearms experiments, in part, were intended to prove the utility of the nascent society and led directly to its royal charter, and that Brouncker, the first president, had appealed

Wenceslaus Hollar, after John Evelyn, frontispiece to Thomas Sprat, *The History of the Royal Society* (1667). Francis Bacon sits on the right, with Brouncker on the left of the bust of King Charles II. Around them are various instruments used in experiments promoted by, or presented to, the society, so the presence of the carbine, or arquebus, on the extreme right is interesting. The firearm seems to be a tacit reminder of the utility of the society to important patrons like the king and Prince Rupert.

directly to the king to be its patron. The first history of the society, published in 1667, shows the scientific instruments used by members on the frontispiece, including a pendulum clock, a telescope and an air pump, along with an arquebus or carbine, as if to remind its important patrons of the practical and useful contribution of the society to an understanding of firearms.[27]

For these experiments Brouncker used 'an engine', meaning some piece of special apparatus – in this case a kind of recoiling carriage – to hold the gun and allow him to observe the motion of the piece on firing. But although he seems to have been more interested in the type of recoil that disturbs the aim, such as a swing to left or right, he also devised an experiment to demonstrate the principle that Newton was to set out more formally as his third law of motion, that action and reaction are opposite and equal. So even before Newton defined those laws, this effect was beginning to be understood, although without Newton's universality and elegance.[28]

Gunners by night, using one of the new combination instruments invented by Leonhard Zubler in *Nova geometrica pyrobolia* (1608).

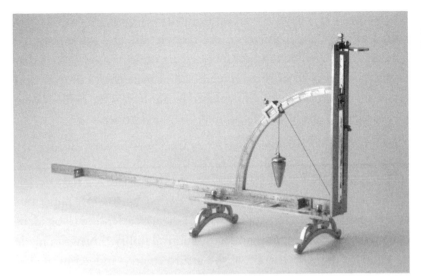

Erasmus Habermel, gunner's quadrant sight and gauge, late 16th century, gilt brass. Curators Jim Bennett and Stephen Johnston considered that 'Habermel's instrument is a tour-de-force whose primary purpose was presumably to grace the collection or cabinet of a noble or wealthy patron.'

The Royal Society was also interested in the velocity of musket bullets ('using Prince Rupert's powder') and asked Robert Hooke, as curator of experiments, to do the tests in 1664.[29] The timing device was a pendulum, held up by a thread that was severed when the bullet exited the muzzle.

These trials show that in England, as in Italy, gunnery was a subject of study for the new experimental science, and also a route to patronage, prestige and support. In 1996 an insightful exhibition called 'The Geometry of War' at the Museum of the History of Science in Oxford set out to explore the status of this science.[30]

Was gunnery, asked the authors Jim Bennett and Stephen Johnston, a practical science or a polite one? Did it belong at war or at court? Was it driven by practice or by theory? Was it characterized by action or by rhetoric? In a sense this was a more nuanced and less choleric formulation of Hall's question about the relationship between gunnery and science.

Some physical evidence lay in the complexity and decoration of the gunnery instruments on display. The basic geometrical tasks for the gunner were estimating distance by measuring the angle of the target from two points (triangulation), measuring height (by a similar operation), and setting the elevation of the cannon. There was also a need to check the diameter of the cannon ball, and sometimes the bore. In time, ingenious and complicated instruments were devised that combined almost all of these functions, but were these complex and beautiful instruments actually deployed by gunners in the field, or were they, perhaps, courtly gifts for gunnery-minded princes?

THE MIND OF GOD

It had been adept of Hessen to select Newton for his 1931 paper but he was, perhaps, the least appropriate of the new scientists to be identified with instrumentalism and with political utility.[31] Newton made no effort to improve the art of the artilleryman – indeed he makes no mention of firearms at all in his theoretical writings and seems to have had no interest in them. And those works, directed as they were to philosophers, made no compromises with utility. Certainly there was nothing in them that was easily accessible at the time to the mill owners and the industrialists cited by Hessen.

But today, when so much research is commercially sponsored, Hessen's thesis seems uncontentious. Half the world's physicists, according to one source, are funded by some form of defence interest. And even if the researchers are people who, in George Clark's words, are driven purely by 'the disinterested desire to know', the university or laboratory where they work may be partly funded by defence contracts, 'Big Oil' or other corporate connections, while the non-commercial funding, perhaps government support or endowments, surely depends on anticipated social or economic utility scryed through complex indicators.

We have come to accept that all thought and experiment is situated in some particular milieu and at some time and place.[32] If guns had not been around 'to challenge the speculation of the naturalist', and if enquirers from Tartaglia to Lord Brouncker had not studied their properties, much of the raw material of observation and inference that Newton used would have been absent.

It was part of Newton's genius to sift, select and assemble what was valid from all the known and codified thought and, together with his own deductions, produce a system of incredible clarity. Certainly, Newton was an instrumental and socially embedded actor when he was Master of the Royal Mint. But might we feel that the reclusive Newton, alone in his rooms in Trinity College, Cambridge, was a 'different Newton' driven only by the 'desire to know'? Perhaps that is naive and some might say that if Newton's works were not socially determined by utility they were, nevertheless, a religious project that sprang from his faith, and intended as an insight into the mind of God. As one of his

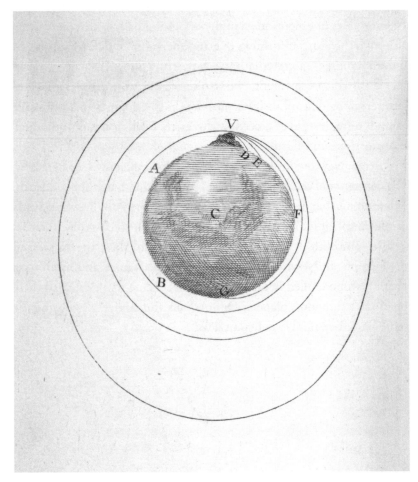

The cannon trajectory illustration in Isaac Newton, *A Treatise of the System of the World* (1728). The passage, in effect, also represents the invention of an artificial satellite, anticipating by nearly three hundred years Sputnik and the International Space Station.

later writings recalls: 'This most beautiful System of the Sun, Planets, and Comets, could only proceed from the counsel and dominion of an intelligent and powerful being . . . This Being governs all things, not as the soul of the world, but as Lord over all.'[33]

But what does a religious, or a social, location say about individual agency, individuality and, above all, about curiosity – one of the most powerful human emotions?

Newton's ambition is revealed by the title of his last work, *The System of the World*, published posthumously in 1728. The final passage in it is a thought experiment in which a projectile is launched with increasing velocity from a mountaintop until it finally enters orbit. Intriguingly, Newton does not mention cannons or cannon balls in this discussion, although the illustrator shows one and the argument clearly implies – indeed requires – a preternaturally powerful gun.

With this experiment, 'Newton escaped from the language of gunnery into that of abstract mechanics, the range of his projectile extends until, instead of descending to earth, it falls forever in an orbital trajectory' around Earth.[34]

Before Newton, the heavens seemed to have their own separate laws. The constancy of celestial motion had seemed unlike anything on Earth, where all motion decays. But ballistics had opened up the whole study of motion, helping to overturn Aristotelian and Renaissance theories and to join both dynamic events on Earth and the patterns seen in the heavens. In Newton's system, 'celestial mechanics' and motion on Earth became unified in one harmonious scheme that explained these phenomena: moons, planets, cannon balls and apples, all obeying the same set of beguilingly coherent laws.

2

THE GUN AND THE FORD

In November 1790 Honoré Blanc, a gunsmith and inventor, astonished French academicians, politicians and military men with a bravura demonstration of a new kind of manufacture. Blanc had produced a thousand gunlocks (the working mechanical parts of a firearm) at an experimental workshop in the donjon (keep) of the Château de Vincennes just outside Paris, and now, in front of these dignitaries, he demonstrated that they were all made from identical interchangeable parts. Selecting pieces at random from bins, Blanc assembled a number of functional muskets to show the perfection of his manufacturing system.[1]

We have become so used to mass production delivering complex and mostly faultless articles, from cars to computers, that the boldness of Blanc's project is now hard to grasp. But, back then, complex mechanical articles like clocks, guns or windmills only worked because of the skill that the craftsman put into each one, assembling, adjusting and tuning each working part one at a time. To create a device that worked repeatedly through the interaction of numerous components, each one relating to the other kinematically and in three dimensions, required a deep, innate understanding of the operating principles of the device. The craftsmen were not just making parts: they were making complete functional ensembles. Therein lay the 'mysteries' of gun-making, of clock-making, or the craft of the shipwrights. All these professions needed a long and attentive apprenticeship. In this earlier industrial world there had been no formal, graphical conventions for engineering drawing and designing, so no way to convey or to specify exactly what a component part should be like, except by imitation and by practice acquired patiently in a workshop. There was no formal way, either, to define a 'fit' or even the quality of a surface finish, except by example, practice, 'feel' and the acquisition of indefinable tacit skills.

Standing within this world of craft, but using new gauges and tools, Blanc pointed to the future and to a world of high-speed machine production. He accompanied his publicity event with a pamphlet to the new revolutionary National Assembly, proposing a state-run workshop that would sweep away the '*ancien régime* of the manufactures' and, running 'to the rhythm of uniform production', would satisfy all France's need for muskets. It would even sweep up and employ the unskilled vagabonds roaming the country.[2]

The phrase *ancien régime*, of course, has an ominous meaning in the context of the Revolution – for who would think that 'the manufactures' could be targets of libertarian disapproval? But even handwork could imply 'privilege' to a revolutionary.

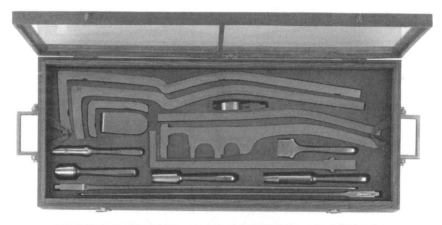

Gauges for manufacture of the Honoré Blanc M1777 musket, 1802–3. They define dimensions of all parts and the positions for all the drillings in the side plates.

THE PRIVILEGE OF THE CRAFTS

In fact, the moral assault on craftsmen was much older than this. The famous *Encyclopédie* of Denis Diderot and Jean le Rond d'Alembert, the great Enlightenment work on the artefactual culture of the time, begun some fifty years earlier, took aim at aristocrats, the clergy and privilege in many forms, but also at the working craftsman and his 'secrecy'.[3]

It is certainly striking that although 'Enlightenment' – the word itself – has such a powerful and positive connotation, the 'Enlightenment project' to cultivate ideal and systematized systems of thought and practical work also implied, or at least foreshadowed, an agenda to unpack and make explicit these embedded, intuitive and ancient craft skills and to attack the private world – and indeed the liberty – of the skilled handworker.

Of course, there was much private knowledge about all the trades, but most of what Diderot considered to be secrets were, in effect, skills and practice, learned by months and years at the workshop bench. How could a mere *philosophe*, however rational, unpick these? The government, Diderot argued, should 'authorise people to go into the factories and shops, to see the craftsmen at their work, to question them, to draw their tools, the machines, and even the premises. All these secrets would have to be divulged, without exception.' He continued with some astonishing polemics:

> I know that this feeling is not shared by everyone. These are narrow minds, deformed souls who are indifferent to the fate of the human race . . . These men insist on being called good citizens, and I consent to this, provided that they permit me to call them *bad men.* To lock up a useful secret is 'despicable' and, moreover, 'to render oneself guilty of a theft from society' . . . These *good citizens* are the most dangerous enemies we have had.[4]

The *Encyclopédie* can therefore be seen both as a 'Doomsday Book' or catalogue of all the existing trades and types of manufacturing

View of a typical 'unreformed' 18th-century craft workshop in Denis Diderot's *Encyclopédie*.

process, but it can also be read as a preparatory text for wresting this privilege and craft knowledge from the guild practitioners in the interests of cheaper goods, the wider diffusion of knowledge and the end of monopolies. An end to craft secrecy, Diderot contended, would free these workmen 'of the illusion, which almost all of them hold, that their art has reached its ultimate perfection. Because they have so little learning they are often inclined to blame the nature of things for defects which exist only in themselves.'

For Diderot, the skilled worker (or 'artist') was clearly a troubling enigma. For though he commended, for example, the 'intelligence, discernment, and consistency' in their 'machines for drawing gold, or making stockings, and in the frames of the braid-makers . . . the drapers, or the silk workers', he cavilled that 'we can hardly find one dozen out of a thousand [of those who practice these mechanical arts] capable of explaining clearly the instruments they use and the products they make.' It must have seemed strange to a savant that these unlettered men were so adept. The solution to all this uncertainty, Diderot divined, was to put the workmen under the direction of a 'philosopher' once his craft secrets had been extracted from him.[5]

GRIBEAUVAL AND SYSTEMATIZATION

The impetus behind Honoré Blanc's attempt to revolutionize musket manufacture reflected similar ideals for systematizing a craft industry and deskilling gun production that had originated with the earlier project of the army officer Jean-Baptiste de Gribeauval to rationalize French artillery.

Before Gribeauval there had been many different types and calibres of cannon in service. From the 1760s he set out to simplify and regularize the equipment. His programme was generally seen as a success and the 'Gribeauvalists' next turned to muskets to unify their design and manufacture.

Gunsmiths were, traditionally, located in independent small craft workshops. To meet large orders, they had to agree and to collaborate. Even if the client was the army, it found it hard to wring more output from the craft producers than they cared to deliver. But these makers were, unfortunately, irreplaceable, because officers and soldiers did not know how to make arms. Only apprentices who had been thoroughly schooled by traditional masters could do the work.

But perhaps, to hardliners, musket makers should be regarded, in effect, as soldiers. Gunsmiths served the army, and soldiers could not fight without them. This was the view taken by Pierre-André Nicolas d'Agoult, who, as supervisor of weapons manufacture for the army at the great industrial centre of Saint-Etienne, jailed dozens of gunsmiths in 1781 for failing, it was alleged, to reach adequate standards. D'Agoult was a tough artilleryman who had twice been wounded – by shell and by bayonet – during the Seven Years' War and presumably had little sympathy for awkward civilians.

However, their imprisonment backfired. The town council took up their cause and had them released, for they were citizens and taxpayers. One response to this was direct army support for Honoré Blanc and his new manufacturing systems. The state would assist Blanc to create a new workshop for arms at Roanne, 50 km (30 mi.) from Saint-Etienne and conveniently far from its troublesome gunsmiths. So Blanc's workshop was more than a technological experiment: it was also a tool to bypass and punish the old-school armourers for their impudence and for their freedom.

Blanc's scheme was a comparatively unsung (and limited) success. He shipped thousands of completed weapons and gunlocks, but we know little about the machinery that he employed for none appears to survive. However, it seems unlikely that the tools could have achieved the required accuracy and repeatability because the improvements to lathes, milling machines and systems needed for fine engineering measurement all lay several decades ahead. Blanc made outstanding contributions to measurement and gauges, but we might guess that there was a high rate of rejection of parts, scrapping components that were 'out of limits', and therefore a substantial cost penalty, as suggested by the fact that the works employed 'adjusters and correctors of . . . gunlock pieces'. There were also 'controllers' doing, in effect, old-style fitting and assembly who were said to have twenty times as much work now compared to the traditional system in which they merely checked the output of the skilled craftsmen gunsmiths. The French state also gave Blanc's factory soft loans, conscript labour and paid a 27 per cent subsidy per gun lock, which took account of the fact that the weapons from this modern, 'rational', but premature, mass production system cost at least 20 per cent more than those from the traditional system it was intended to displace.[6] This cost penalty alone would explain why this ideal of standardized production was not fully achieved and why the model of Blanc's workshop did not spread to other enterprises. By 1800 Napoleon's director of artillery had closed it down and so, as we shall see, this ideal gun-making system initiated by Honoré Blanc only came to fruition much later, and in America. Known generally there as 'the armory system', it resulted from immense expenditure, decades of experiment and many improvements to machine tools and to measurement, all largely pioneered in the United States and financed from government funds. As with many radical technical innovations, only weapons development seems to have the exceptional power to inspire the research needed and to underwrite the huge cost of such a speculative long-range project.

TIME THRIFT AND EARLY INDUSTRIAL CAPITALISM

The key elements in the armoury system would include the extensive use of machinery and the strict division of labour, ideally reducing each worker's task to a single, repetitive operation, as Blanc's work had anticipated. For Karl Marx, writing in the *Communist Manifesto* in 1848, it was exactly these elements that had robbed work of all its individual character, 'and, consequently, all charm for the workman'. To these factors, of course, should be added the steam engine and the time clock, the metronomes of industrial rhythm that Marx thought so important.

This is the view that has been adopted widely by social historians, but in England, Marx's prime example of a state that embraced the deployment of capital for profit and production, the desire to discipline and control the work process came long before the establishment of factories and mills equipped with automatic machinery and steam power. E. P. Thompson, in his powerful essay 'Time, Work-discipline and Industrial Capitalism', quotes a telling letter from 1681 on the then unmechanized British textile trades:

> When the frame-work knitters or makers of silk-stockings had a great price for their work, they have been observed seldom to work on Mondays and Tuesdays but to spend most of their time at the ale-house or nine-pins . . . The weavers, it is common with them to be drunk on Monday, to have their headaches on Tuesday, and their tools out of order on Wednesday.[7]

Thompson suggests that 'alternate bouts of intense labour and idleness' are typical 'wherever men were in control of their own working lives', and still persists, he notes, 'among some self-employed – artists, writers . . . and perhaps also with students'.[8]

As industry became more centralized and systematized, 'time became currency' and it was 'not passed, it was spent'. Indeed the 'propaganda of time thrift' continued and intensified as mechanization and centralization took hold.[9] The problem of leisure, Thompson shows, was acutely

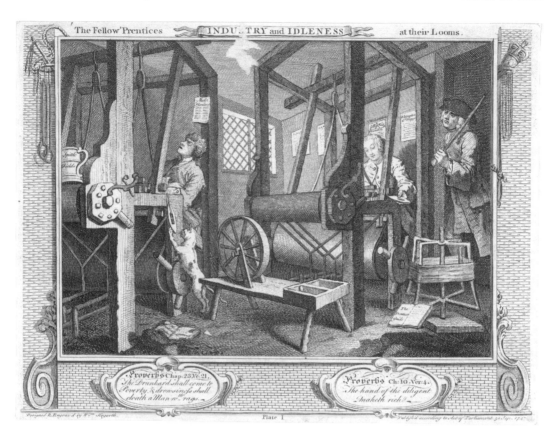

William Hogarth, 'The Fellow 'Prentices at their Looms', 1747, in the *Industry and Idleness* series. The quotation from the Book of Proverbs, below the indolent apprentice on the left with a pot of ale, reads: 'the drunkard shall come to poverty.' For his dutiful colleague, 'the hand of the diligent maketh rich.'

troubling to moralists in the early Industrial Revolution, with one writer in 1821 regretting that manual workers were often left with several hours a day 'to be spent nearly as they please. And in what manner . . . is this precious time expended by those of no mental cultivation?' The answer, it seemed, was to give in to 'utter vacancy and torpor' on some bench or hillock, or to gather in groups by the wayside ready to practice 'gross jocularity', impertinence, 'or some jeering scurrility at the expense of persons going by'.[10]

Somehow, in the march from feudalism to industrialization, certain trades had arisen with the power to control their own output and their own labour – to dictate, in effect, the terms and the intensity with which they would work. It was a privilege and a liberty that merchants, monopolists, moralists and social improvers increasingly resented.

This was a pre-industrial, eighteenth-century contest about who should control the labour process.[11] It arose because practical people, used to working with metals, materials and mechanisms, could deploy their intelligence, and their skill, for a while at least, in areas of work and commerce that merchants and financiers could not understand well enough to penetrate and to control. These were the kind of people who had built the first town and cathedral clocks, often as peripatetic crafts-men going from town to town, taking on contracts to build these important and – as they came to be seen – socially necessary new devices. Theirs was the kind of intelligence that developed house clocks, watches, guns of all kinds, and could forge and form essential household things: knives, pans, locks and scissors that would cut and would last.

The prejudice of the eighteenth-century philosopher against the craftsman is also apparent in the work of Adam Smith. In an early draft for part of *The Wealth of Nations* he suggested, for example, that water- and windmills 'were due to no work man of any kind, but a philosopher . . . one of those people whose trade it is not to do any thing but to observe every thing'.[12] The truth was almost absurdly at odds with his view. Perhaps classical Greece was different, for its pre-eminent thinkers had been interested in mechanisms in the broadest sense.[13] But almost all the subtle developments of practical machinery from Roman times and through the Middle Ages had been due to 'canny men' – unlettered men – and it is probably true that no philosopher in most of Europe had been responsible for any improvements in mechanism whatsoever from the Middle Ages until the dawn of the Industrial Revolution.

Most improvements arose organically within all these professions. Naturally, many millwrights – or clockmakers for that matter – were content to repeat the sound designs they had been taught. But some were more imaginative and experimental, and hence responsible for the subtle evolution of these machines. These exceptional craftsmen, for instance, perfected the gearing that drove the wheels of watermills carrying a large amount of power (before the mathematical theory for gear shapes had arrived). They designed the adjustable sluices to regulate these mills (and the schemes for river management that lasted into contemporary times until people forgot how to use them). They invented windmills that could swivel cleverly to best meet the wind as it shifted (post mills). They devised sails for windmills, too, that could be taken in or reefed so that the mill would not be overpowered in a gale. It was an age of invention before 'inventors' became defined and celebrated. In an era before personalization and priority, these original minds were only recognized in their own close communities and their

Fra Raffaello da Brescia, detail from inlaid panel of clock with a swinging foliot (the curved beam seen under the bell), which keeps the time, c. 1513–37. The inventor of the foliot is unknown, though it is one of the greatest mechanical discoveries of the late Middle Ages.

names are forgotten. Even the inventor of the foliot – the swinging beam that made the first proper mechanical clocks possible – is unknown, although a later historian recorded that if we knew his name 'he would be worthy of all our praise.'

But the system of division of labour, the atomization of work tasks, which Marx perhaps rightly blamed for robbing work of 'all charm', was partly an invention of the independent craftsmen themselves. If you had been in a watchmaking area like the Clerkenwell district of London in the late eighteenth century, you would have been struck by the sight of porters bearing trays and boxes fitted with special compartments, scurrying up tenement stairs into upper floors and attics or into workshops built out behind the houses to collect the diverse parts of watches and to carry them from one specialist to another. One man might make only hairsprings for balance wheels, some cut wheels (gears in engineering parlance), some painted dials, others just cut and blued the hands. Some fitted up the movements with all their working parts before it was married to the watch case – and that too came from another craftsman. Even the secret springs that open and lock the front and back of these cases came from specialists. The reason for this ruthless subdivision was speed. No doubt during their apprenticeships such men had learned many skills and many of these artists could have made the whole watch themselves, but when an apprentice, or his workmates, noticed that he had a special aptitude or 'touch' there was a natural encouragement to specialize in the interest of speed and output.

All these watch parts were incredibly demanding to make, needed the most delicate and practised touch, were impeccably detailed and finished, and were made almost at the limits of human vision. A watch dial painter, for example, must work with unerring movements and at tiny scale. One wrong stroke – even the last one – condemns the whole job. At least thirty trades were involved in making an English pocket watch.

These men did not need Henry Ford to tell them about the atomization of labour for they knew that they could only get the speed of their output up and aspire to a living wage by ruthless specialization, so they came to know their tools, their processes and their materials blindfold and so, to maximize earnings, these craftsmen learned to specialize. Between them that army of porters moved the components and partly built watches around the neighbourhood to keep this great diversified trade flowing smoothly, producing a huge output of beautifully made timepieces.

This style of manufacture has largely been forgotten because it was so diffuse. For the most part it has vanished without trace for, unlike Ford, Austin and Fiat, it left few enduring monuments in architecture. Its workshops were the tenements of old London, in areas like Spitalfields or Clerkenwell, or the terraced houses of Birmingham's jewellery quarter.[14] It was, indeed, 'mass production before the factory'.

A finished watch movement from Prescot, the great Lancashire watch centre, c. 1870. Many individuals in dispersed workshops collaborated to bring the movement to this state. It then had another journey in this purpose-made box to the finisher who would fit it to a case, made by yet another specialist, and perhaps put a proprietary name on it.

THE BIRMINGHAM GUN TRADE AND ITS CRITICS

In spite of the power and subtlety of these organically evolved manu-facturing systems, the new pattern of mass production located in purpose-built and heavily capitalized factories would inevitably have arrived, although it was the gun, and the state's requirement for weap-ons, that added impetus to the search for a new, integrated system of production.

By the 1850s concerns about the supply of British weapons and the state of Britain's arms supplies focused on the great Birmingham gun trade. It was a strange replay of the contests over arms production seen in France some sixty years before.

Birmingham, 'the city of a thousand trades', was the principal source of firearms. It epitomized the flexible and dispersed network of spe-cialists that characterized the early industrial world and it had been an efficient producer to survive so long. But its adversaries argued that the trade was slow, awkward and undercapitalized.

The Crimean War exposed a problem with the supply of military weapons. The fundamental and traditional structure of the trade con-sisted of dividing operations between specialists who were their own masters. This seemed profoundly objectionable to modernizers. A self-employed barrel filer could make a dozen barrels for you, or could choose to take a day off in the pub, or at the races. And so, 'as part of an argument for greater mechanisation . . . production in small work-shops was widely condemned as both economically inefficient and an encouragement to working class immorality.'[15]

To the government critics, the Birmingham gun trade seemed to be a relic of the eighteenth century that had strayed impertinently into the new, modern, nineteenth century and witnesses to the 1854 Parliamentary Select Committee on the Manufacture of Small Arms focused on its 'archaic nature'. The ideal model, implicitly, was the new and integrated American system. One committee member demanded to know 'why the manufacturers of Birmingham are so much at the mercy of their men: if they have that quantity of machinery that I think is applicable to gunmaking they ought to be quite independent of those men and not knuckling down to them as they are.'[16]

The unpalatable truth was that these workers were not 'their men' at all. The gun trade was largely a constellation of small proprietors, each with their own workshop and a few employees – people often known in the Midlands metal trades as 'small masters'. And there were many free individual craftsmen, all specializing in particular parts or a process for the gun. Some filed parts of the lock, some finished barrels, some made gunstocks and so on. It was a fascinating ecology. There were

Birmingham, 'the city of a thousand trades', in the late 19th century, drawn by Percival Skelton.

independent metalworkers who often owned nothing more than a work-bench, a leather apron and a couple of pounds' worth of tools. Some owned almost nothing but their skill and rented 'shopping', as it was known – a single place at a workbench or a blacksmith's hearth. Fifty-one different Birmingham gun trades were listed in the early 1800s.[17]

The usual process was that when a substantial government contract was to be fulfilled it would be taken on by a principal master or a merchant (who, confusingly, probably also styled himself a 'gunmaker'). Then a large number of meetings, negotiations and conversations were needed with all these dispersed craftsmen-owners in order to agree final prices and delivery times for their own special contributions.

In spite of the alleged backwardness of this style of Birmingham production, output increased fivefold between 1803 and 1815 without larger firms being needed. It had not become more mechanized, or consolidated into unitary factories on the American pattern, because government expenditure had been much less, and orders for arms had been sporadic and patchy. The problem, the gunmakers contended, was a lack of consistency and lack of foresight from government.

The highly integrated American armoury sprang from quite different economic conditions and from different funding opportunities. America had a relentless appetite for arms and a government that was prepared to capitalize an expensive experiment in production. But the model – or the ideal – of the American factory was a useful rhetorical device in the 'protracted struggle in which wage-earners gradually lost much of their ability to control the work process', to choose when to work, or not, and to enjoy, until then, a surprising, and provocative, degree of autonomy.[18]

But the rhetoric of modernity had its own momentum and the American example also helped sustain the long-running discourse about 'working class immorality'. Indeed, the link between mechanization and 'moral advance' seemed to be one of the great attractions of American practice and when a second British commission visited America to inspect the Springfield and Harpers Ferry armories it reported on 'the discipline and sobriety of the employed'.[19]

Whitworth's stand at the Great Exhibition of 1851, drawn by Louis Haghe.

Perhaps the last act in this struggle was the decision to purchase American machinery for Britain to help expand production in the government-owned Royal Arsenal at Enfield. Partly in response, Birmingham too developed a more unified privately capitalized production system with the formation of BSA (the Birmingham Small Arms Company), created in 1861 by a group of gunmakers in order to invest in new machinery and an integrated factory.

THE AMERICAN SYSTEM OF PRODUCTION

But how did American practices become the standard that Britain looked to in order to reproach its own arms manufacturers? After all, at the Great Exhibition of 1851, Britain boasted manufacturers like Joseph Whitworth, whose machine tools and new exact measuring instruments had impressed the world. Whitworth built the kind of universal metal-working tools that engineered the empire, for they could make anything from a cotton spinning machine to a locomotive – if the men were there who knew how to use them.

The 'American system' had a different aim to British engineering practice: it set out to devise whole suites of special single-purpose tools, each making only one subcomponent, or doing only one job, marshalled in factories designed to make only one type of product. It was the gun that was the impetus for devising such a complex and expensive system.

The kind of organization that resulted is often characterized as 'deskilling' production, but that is not really true. It certainly allows the less skilled or unskilled worker to have a large role in production but actually it is a 'skill multiplier'. Genuine craftsmen are still needed to devise, to set up and to adjust the production machinery but now they are found in the 'holy of holies' of the mass-production factory – the tool room – from whence they emerge to adjust, repair and set the production machinery.

In consequence, the toolmakers became a race apart, entirely different to the operatives who ran the machines or worked on the line. In the heyday of the great car companies, for example, a 'toolroom job' implied the highest standards that could be achieved, and the toolmakers themselves became a kind of industrial aristocracy, a step never foreseen by Denis Diderot or Adam Smith.

Some historians have suggested that it was the comparative shortage of skilled engineers, and the need to use them efficiently, that led to this new American system. Others consider that it was the large American market that justified investment in the new systems, although the British and American populations were roughly equivalent in size at the time.[20] What seems inescapable, though, is that the underpinnings of the system were not solely economic but derived from a kind of idealism implicit in the search for rational and systematic gun manufacture. It was this that provided the foundations for this new American style of manufacture.

One key was that, following Blanc's demonstrations in France in 1790, the new concept of the idealized mass production of weapons quickly took root in the new American republic, stimulated by letters sent home by Thomas Jefferson, as Minister (ambassador) in Paris. The project appealed to the United States military because it implied faster assembly and more consistent performance, but also promised firearms that could be repaired more easily in the field and even, if necessary, cannibalized when damaged for replacement parts. Government money began to pour into systems for making weapons the new way, both to government arsenals, like the armories at Springfield and at Harpers Ferry, but also to private contractors like Eli Whitney.

In fact, the American search for interchangeability proved far more arduous than almost anyone expected and the whole project makes an intriguing philosophical comment on the problem of knowledge, for though the 'possessive' traditional craftsman (as characterized by Diderot) certainly had his secrets and knew a huge amount, he did not know how to systematize and diffuse this knowledge to others, except by example and tutelage. There was practice, art and skill, but no codified set of atomistic 'secrets' that he could impart. The mass-made gun looked much the same, and did the same job, but it was really a new kind of article that differed profoundly in its conception from the craftsman's weapon.

The phrase 'tacit knowledge' is often used in discussing the intuitive skill of the traditional craftsman, but the difficult challenge of describing this kind of knowledge is seldom attempted and indeed may be impossible, except in a literary way.[21] Here, we try to characterize it in reverse, by reviewing some of the ideas and practices that had to be devised to replace this knowledge and practice. The skill of hand and eye, the sense of 'feel' and observation when fitting subassemblies together, the intuitive and internalized mental design picture held by the craftsman – all these had to be replaced by newly invented systematic techniques and new geometrical concepts such as 'the bearing point' (we would say now a 'datum') to which all the other surfaces, holes or functional elements on a component were to measure and relate in a precise way.

Today, the unambiguous definition of a three-dimensional object by drawings (whether on paper or on computer) seems a necessary and natural step in design and manufacture, but it was not done earlier in the craft era of production. Although architecture had long used formalized drawings, smaller but complex mechanical items like clocks,

Manufacturing muskets
in the USA,
in *Harper's Weekly*,
21 September 1861.

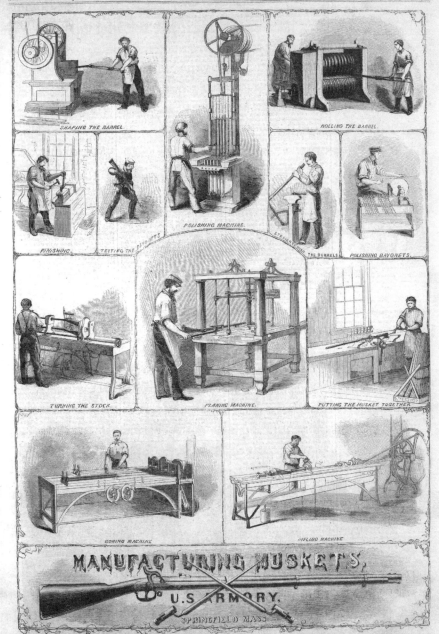

SHAPING THE BARREL.

ROLLING THE BARREL.

POLISHING MACHINE.

FINISHING.   TESTING THE BAYONETS.   STRAIGHTENING THE BARRELS.   POLISHING BAYONETS.

TURNING THE STOCK.   PLANING MACHINE.   PUTTING THE MUSKET TOGETHER.

BORING MACHINE.   RIFLING MACHINE.

MANUFACTURING MUSKETS,
U.S. ARMORY.
SPRINGFIELD MASS.

guns and door locks evolved incrementally from preceding types and lived in the mind of their creators. Occasionally, too, models were used, often to promote an idea, to patent it or to explain. Back then, the three-dimensional article had primacy over descriptive, two-dimensional drawings, which usually were created after the act of invention and creation (if they existed at all), often for reference works and 'Cyclopedias'. So, for factory production to emerge, a whole new graphical language of engineering drawing had to be devised, with new drawing conventions. There were various semi-perspective techniques emerging, such as the 'first angle projection', and notations to fully represent all the details and dimensions of every part to the machinist.

The aim of the new armoury system, as we have seen, was to achieve consistency in individual components to allow rapid assembly without all the usual fettling and fitting. However, there was a snag. Even with the new production machinery that was being devised, it became clear that parts with ideal, invariable dimensions were still not fully achievable since machine tools wear, change and even flex as they cut, stamp or forge parts. There will also be inevitable dimensional 'creep', as well as a random statistical variation in components. This is a problem, since the whole point of standardization is to reduce the dependence on skill and judgement during final assembly; the craftsman is no longer supposed to be there to match parts together.

One solution is through measurement. Though micrometers and gauges accurate to 1/1000th of an inch (25 microns) or better were spreading into the workshops through the nineteenth century, designers and engineers had to evolve a new understanding to use this new potential for high accuracy.

What was needed was a 'philosophy of gauging', which meant formalizing a system to determine what size ranges ('limits' or 'tolerances') were acceptable. This presented a novel intellectual and practical problem, which took time and experiment. All the individual size limits for components must be considered in the context of the entire finished machine, understanding the interaction between each part and its neighbours and following the whole chain of these interactions

American-made hand micrometer, 1870s. Although large bench micrometers were known, it now became possible for individual machinists on the shop floor to have a personal reference accurate to 1/1000th of an inch or better.

between parts in the device through each functional step. The reason was that a pair of parts might work together over a range of allowable sizes, but a more complex assembly of many parts that were all, by chance, say, at the maximum permitted size could add up to an accumulation of tolerances that would make the whole assembly unworkable. This, in part, was the kind of 'secret' that the old gunsmiths knew, but did not have the language to say.

Initially, true interchangeability was expensive. But the American government could afford to pay more for effectively identical or interchangeable weapons than most private customers. Nevertheless, the experiment to attain this ideal, needing over forty years of government-sponsored development, unintentionally subsidized the progress of American manufacture in general. The consequence was a new technique of amazing power, now often known as 'the American system of mass production'.[22]

The new technique (or the promise of it) was also an avenue of self-advancement for many engineers. Just as Honoré Blanc had invited dignitaries to disassemble and reassemble his weapons to prove their perfection and identicality, so Eli Whitney later placed samples in the hands of U.S. government and military representatives, inviting them to try the same test to prove the supposed perfection of his mechanized processes.

The sleight of hand lay in the fact that no one knew how much preparation had gone into the selection of these special parts for these special demonstration weapons, since this piece of theatre was almost certainly accompanied, privately, by exceptional measures in gauging all the parts and by trial assembly, way beyond what would have been economically practical in real production. This view is supported by independent comments that Whitney's factory, at the time, contained 'only the simplest, least expensive equipment'.[23] Nevertheless, Whitney secured the contracts that kept him afloat, while inspectors came to realize that they had to measure parts taken at random. The American armoury project, however, definitely succeeded and formed the milieu in which, as David Hounshell has described, Yankee mechanics 'worked out their ideas and then moved on to exploit them in the outside world'.[24] In fact, Eli Whitney's cousin Amos, also an eminent inventor for the armament and other industries, went on with his colleague Francis Pratt to found the machine tool company that lives on today as Pratt & Whitney, one of the pre-eminent makers of jet engines in the world.

MOTOR CITY: A MILLION GROANING SINNERS DRAGGED INTO HELL

The huge sums that the American government had poured into the armoury project soon started to provide an enormous uplift to the whole of American manufacturing, although that had not been the original intention. It was a classic example of the kind of economic 'pump priming' that politicians and governments often try to achieve, though often with uncertain results. Steadily, 'armory practice' became a synonym for the finest standards in production engineering and its methods began to diffuse into other types of manufacturing, although they were not always fully understood. Soon 'armory men' were bringing a subtler understanding of measurement, design definition and the role of size limits or tolerances to American factories, which were starting to make everything from typewriters to combine harvesters.

Of course, the system was not always understood perfectly at first. For example, the Singer Sewing Machine Company glimpsed the importance of true measurements and gauging, but started by attempting to make only perfectly sized or 'ideal' parts, without understanding how unattainable these were. In consequence it had to resort to a high scrap rate and to use expert, selective assembly: really a variant of the pre-existing (some said 'English') craft practice of engineering. But this was just a hiccup. Waltham watch factories near Boston showed how the new systems could be applied to make a complicated device that previously took hours of specialist labour.

Cyrus McCormick's enormous new factory plant in Chicago also perfected mass production to supply the enormous and growing wheat fields of the Midwest with reapers and agricultural machinery. But it was in the field of automobile manufacture that the new techniques had their most public success. Armoury men made a timely arrival in Detroit when Henry Ford was trying a new experiment in car production,

In 1885 the Waltham Watch Company sent a piece of industrial theatre – a miniature production line – to the International Inventions Exhibition in London. The operatives formed and assembled parts sequentially on a flow line to demonstrate the superiority of the system over European methods.

for mass assembly by his largely unskilled labour force would have been impossible without repeatability and dimensional control. The armoury system was not, in itself, mass production, but its principles of dimensional control, measurement and repeatability were the essential precursors for it.

Ford's Model T was the sturdy, well-priced car that motorized America. And although it was a utilitarian object, it had high quality in its design, assembly and metallurgy that gave it long life in adverse environments and with basic maintenance. Though not fast, it had the flexibility, toughness and high ground clearance suited to an age when much of the road network was still potholed and unpaved.

The appropriateness of its design for its day also justified the creation of Henry Ford's vast plants and a huge production run of 15 million cars over almost twenty years (a statistic only rivalled many years later by the Volkswagen Beetle). This enormous level of investment in integrated factories was justified because Ford was perhaps the first to achieve the levels of quality, consistency, but above all, suitability of the car itself for the American landscape.

Ford cars, in fact, could not have been made so cheaply at any earlier point in time, for several historical currents had to come together.

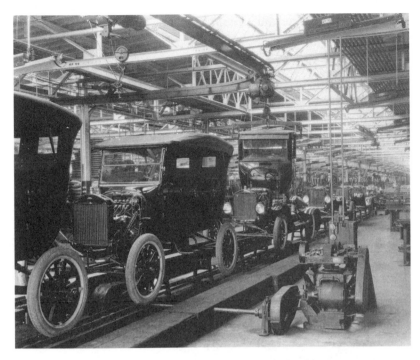

The classical image of 20th-century modernity – Model T Fords on an unstoppable flow line.

Albert Kahn's 1910 Highland Park plant in November 1914, purpose built for Ford's production methods.

And though New England armoury practice played a part, there was much more. 'Moving the work to the men' was one ingredient and Ford once suggested that the overhead conveyor 'disassembly' lines of the Chicago butchers (meatpackers) were the inspiration. But this throwaway remark obscured the fact that conveyor belts were already part of the industrial milieu in the USA.

Another ingredient was the ruthless subdivision of labour, epitomized in Henry Ford's rubric: 'the man who places a part does not fasten it . . . The man who puts in a bolt does not put on the nut; the man who puts on the nut does not tighten it.'[25]

Many have argued for the role of F. W. Taylor and his new study of 'scientific management' in this transformation, but the Ford plant was far more subtle and organic than he could have arranged. While Taylor studied human actions in the individual 'work steps' to optimize speed and economy of movement, and certainly made a contribution to the refinement of individual tasks, Ford production engineers deployed a deep understanding of engineering possibilities, which Taylor did not possess. They redesigned parts to cut out process steps or to reduce criticality in particular dimensions, experimented with new materials and faster metal-forming techniques, and organized the sequencing of operations and the precise location of every machine tool in the plant.

Characteristically, Henry Ford claimed to have discovered the whole technique of mass production by himself, though Charles Sorensen, one of his experts, was explicit in crediting the broad company team:

Layout of machines in Horace Lucien Arnold and Fay Leone Faurote, *Ford Methods and the Ford Shops* (1919).

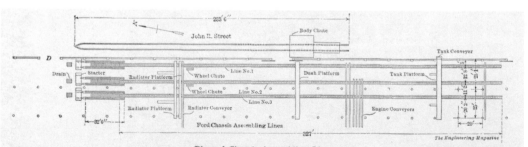

Plan of Chassis-Assembling Lines

The chassis assemblies begin at the south (right-hand) end, and move to the north (left-hand) end, under the overhead gasoline-tank platform, the motor-carrying chain-hoist tracks, the dash assembly platform and the radiator platform. They then take the wheels, run on the wheels on roller frames over the pit where a workman caps the front-axle bracing globe, and then down a short incline onto the motor-starting drive for the rear wheels. Then the chassis is driven under its own power, through the door, *D*, and on the John R street track to the southward

Henry Ford had no ideas on mass production. He wanted to build a lot of autos. He was determined but, like everyone else at that time, he didn't know how. In later years he was glorified as the originator of the mass production idea. Far from it; he just grew into it like the rest of us. The essential tools and the final assembly line with its many integrated feeders resulted from an organization that was continually experimenting and improvising.[26]

The Model T was much more than transportation, for it embodies Henry Ford's claim to have invented an entirely new method of production that was economical and prolific. 'I do not consider the machines that bear my name simply as machines,' he proclaimed:

If that was all there was to it I would be doing something else. I take them as concrete evidence of the working out of a theory of business which I hope is more than a theory of business – a theory which looks forward to making this world a better place to live.[27]

Buoyed up by success and self-esteem, Ford blundered beyond the auto industry, trying his hand at domestic politics, antisemitic propaganda, a world peace initiative and, in 1924, allowed himself to be discussed as a possible presidential candidate. But though President Calvin Coolidge (the Christian name seems significant) was no doubt thinking of Ford when he said 'the man who builds a factory builds a temple', the actual experience of work in a Ford-style factory was oppressive to most employees 'on the line', and was responsible, in part, for the long period of union activism in the post-war era that helped contribute to the decline of the original 'motowns', whether in Detroit, Michigan, or Birmingham, England.

The advent of mass manufacture on the Ford pattern had created a newly affluent working class that could, in effect, afford the products of its own labour. The conditions of work opened up the ongoing dialectic of the production line, which made car manufacture a particularly contested arena for industrial relations. A contemporary observer of Ford's new factory system wrote that 'the din of its motors and its mechanisms was like listening to a million pigs dying . . . [or] a million groaning sinners as they are dragged into hell.'[28]

FORDISM AND THE WORLD

In 1912 Giovanni Agnelli returned to Turin from a visit to America. The former Piedmontese cavalry officer, now the visionary chief of FIAT (Fabbrica Italiana Automobili Torino) had gone there in particular to see Ford's Highland Park factory, declaring: 'I wanted to see for myself the danger that is threatening.'[29]

He saw, in Detroit, the extraordinary vertical integration of production at Henry Ford's Highland Park plant. Steel became parts, parts became cars, and the manufacturing cost per car was almost half that of Fiat. Agnelli immediately started planning a similar system for Italy.

Agnelli and Fiat were not the only car makers to follow the path to Detroit and to adopt Ford doctrines. The visit was to be just one of many, down the years, from the world's car makers who came to marvel at the perfect integration of Ford's systems, the seemingly unstoppable flow of parts and cars, and to learn the principles of Ford's rational and highly honed system.

In one sense they hardly needed to come at all, except to witness the sheer industrial drama of the Ford production lines. The reason was that Henry Ford, as an industrial evangelist, was keen on the widest dissemination of his ideas and techniques. For example, from about 1910 he invited the engineer and writer Horace Lucien Arnold to study Ford methods and to publish them as a series of articles in the New York-based *Engineering Magazine* ('devoted to industrial progress'). These were gathered together and culminated in the masterly 1919 work *Ford Methods and the Ford Shops*, which set out the Ford assembly techniques in the finest detail. It introduced the principles of the moving assembly line to the wider world, explaining the detailed art of integrating production, and the importance of accuracy and of gauging dimensions.[30]

Moreover, there were annual pamphlets such as *Factory Facts from Ford*, and articles on assembly methods in the *Ford Times* newsletter. Of course, the novelty, and the immensity, of the Ford enterprise attracted wider coverage in the general press, while Ford also spread news of its achievements through its own in-house film unit. This made documentaries on a wide range of general interest subjects for public circulation, although a good proportion were about Ford systems and Ford news. It was, for a time, the biggest film unit in America.

On his return to Italy, Agnelli's American revelation began to transform the nature of Fiat and planning started for the immense Lingotto plant, an extraordinary new factory in Turin that was to be the most direct homage to Ford's techniques and his Highland Park plant to be realized anywhere in the world. 'Don't expect to be invited into the *Biennale* [of architecture],' Agnelli told the engineer-architect Giacomo Mattè-Trucco when commissioning him to design it. 'No aesthetic preoccupations – that's how you must work for industry.'[31]

When the First World War broke out a healthy demand from Allied armies for Fiat trucks helped bankroll the construction of the new building. What arose in Lingotto, then a suburb of Turin, was an enormous factory five storeys high and several city blocks long, using a vast number of identical repeating elements – columns, ceiling beams and huge glazed window apertures – and closely following the 'concrete daylight' formula established in Detroit by Ford's architect, Albert Kahn. But it did have poetic and original features of its own, particularly the two elegant spiral ramps at each end for transporting cars and parts between floors, with the roadway supported on slim radiating, fan-shaped beams, and a more fantastical touch: the oval test track on the roof.

The track, contrary to myth, was not meant for hurtling around or for racing. Only a lunatic would risk missing a corner to launch themselves off the oval five floors up in the air. Rather, it was intended for relatively sedate tests of assembled cars on brakes, steering, checking all the gears for engagement and so on, before shipping. However, it is rather doubtful that the track ever saw much use, apart from its frequent appearance in publicity shots.

Lingotto in Turin –
the biggest monument
to Fordism outside
America, albeit with
some wonderful Italian
touches: the striking fan
vaulting over the internal
ramps and the famous
rooftop test track.

Many Italians were impressed by Lingotto, seeing it as proud evidence of the nation's increasing industrial prowess, though some critics sensed that Fordism was antithetical both to industrial workers and to precious northern Italian traditions, particularly to craft skill and virtuoso handwork with metal. To such critics, Lingotto was simply 'an island of America', though it was one that also helped to show that Fordism could be transplanted around the world.[32]

Contrary to Agnelli's prediction that the architectural establishment would reject the building, Le Corbusier visited several times and saw it as 'certainly one of the most impressive spectacles of industry . . . a Florentine work, punctual, limpid, clear'.[33] It is not fanciful to see in it an inspiration for the repeating modules in Le Corbusier's own 1947 design for L'Unité d'Habitation in Marseilles, and also to see the use of the test track as a suggestion for the running track and swimming pool on the roof of Le Corbusier's own vertical town. So was it Ford, not architectural theory, that made homes become, for some designers at least, 'machines for living in'?

With the help of Lingotto, Fiat emerged as a major, low-cost European maker and the linchpin of Italian industry during the 1920s and '30s. After the Second World War it revived this position with intelligently engineered, good-value cars under the design leadership of Dante Giacosa. This approach was epitomized by the Fiat Cinquecento, perhaps post-war Europe's own equivalent of the Model T and still one of the supreme automotive achievements in terms of its 'package efficiency'. Fiat, moreover, proved that Fordism was not confined to Detroit. It could be exported round the world.

Both Highland Park and Lingotto, however, showed the limits of tall multi-storey factories. Eventually, neither structure proved to be the best way to build cars, for these modernist concrete temples were soon found to be comparatively inflexible and unsympathetic to improvements in machine tools, new production techniques or changes to the model of car being built.

Sadly, the next generation of car plants were not to become lasting industrial monuments but would consist of architecturally humdrum single-storey sheds that could spread out in a linear way across open country in response to new processes, new models and so on. Ford himself showed the way with his next enterprise, the bravura River

Le Corbusier's Unité d'Habitation in Marseilles – the mass production aesthetic transposed to domestic architecture.

Rouge plant. The Rouge site was 2.5 km (1½ mi.) long with some ninety buildings. Production there went from raw iron ore, to steel, then car components, and then finally assembly of the complete Model A – Ford's new model. It was 'an industrial city . . . and industrial marvel, the largest concentration of machinery and labour anywhere in the world'.[34]

Similarly, by the 1930s Fiat was planning the Mirafiori plant on a new green-field site situated outside Turin. There was still an impressive five-storey facade, but this frontage held only offices. The actual work of car production took place in long, single-storey, pent-roofed buildings behind it, because production planners found that these structures suited assembly lines best. This new utilitarian architecture allowed expansion longitudinally or sideways and the saw-toothed roof profile of the sheds became typical of car plants around the world.

The change in architectural style hinted at a deep contradiction in Fordism and in mass production in general. One major key to efficiency is the single-purpose machine. If the component is invariable, each machine needs no adjustment or tool changes beyond maintenance and maintaining its accuracy throughout the thousands of repetitions it has to perform. Another key advantage, back then, was that such machines ensured that their operators had the most atomized industrial tasks.

This rigidity brings tremendous cost advantages when the car does not change, and Henry Ford seemed to think that with the Model T he had created an almost eternal product. Certainly, its qualities and its practicality in the emerging age of the automobile gave it a uniquely long run, but in time new roads, higher speeds and advanced models from other makers left it behind. To switch production to the replacement Model A Ford in 1927 took a vast convulsion, closing the production lines for six months with machines being hauled out and replaced wholesale, a cost in money and human effort that manufacturers less committed to specialization did not have to bear.[35] The cost of all this was not borne by the company alone. Anecdotally, some 60,000 Ford workers were said to have been laid off during the changeover. In more modern times, though, this kind of management was no longer on option: in 1949 *Life* magazine ran 'An Advertisement of the Ford Motor Company' claiming that 'Ford is trying to lick a major problem – big layoffs for model change-over' and boasting 'steadier planning and more security for Ford employees . . . better economic health for the whole nation. That's the Ford way.'[36]

But though the flexibility of General Motors in introducing innovations and new models had been the factor that forced Ford to make the changeover to the new Model A, Henry Ford still did not subscribe to the new twentieth-century habit of repetitive consumption, remaining an unrepentant advocate of the standard product and of long, unchanging production runs.[37] The new Model A Ford, he hoped, would prove 'so strong and so well made that no one ought ever to have to buy another one'.[38]

This tension between rigid, purpose-made tools and greater freedom and flexibility is the central conundrum at the heart of mass production,

The Fiat Mirafiori plant, built after the Second World War. The humdrum fast-build single-storey sheds of modern car factories reveal the tension between standardization and flexibility in production line design.

one which other manufacturers have struggled constantly to unpick. The 'one car line' will, almost inevitably, make a cheaper product, though the enormous cost of this inflexible tooling brings risks too. If the market rejects the car, the company may face an almost existential threat.

JAPAN AND FLEXIBILITY

In the 1950s, among the many industrialists who continued to visit Ford's factories, Eiji Toyoda, nephew of Sakichi Toyoda, founder of the Toyoda loom works, an inventive Japanese textile machinery company now branching out into automobiles branded Toyota, came to Detroit. He saw the huge flows of material and awesome systems of organization. But he came away, quite humbly, believing Toyota could do as well, if not better. And his colleague, the engineer Taiichi Ohno, also saw the same astonishing feats of integration in Detroit, but also waste, delay, inflexibility and a kind of organizational fossilization.

In spite of decades of refinement, the Toyota men did not believe that the American system had reached the limits of efficiency. Where most observers saw power and irresistible forces of production, the Toyota men saw profligacy – even waste – and set out to reform mass production.

Many aspects of the Japanese system that they would help to evolve seemed almost spiritual – waste was abhorred because the monetary worth of scrapped parts was money that the company could never have back. It was a cost to the nation, and the planet, too. And the huge parts inventories that the u.s. companies maintained so that the line never stopped were anathema as well. American companies, with their enormous stocks of components, were absorbing their own capital in financing their production and in warehousing them.

Ohno, who has been widely acknowledged as the main architect of lean production, gnomically pronounced that the larger the inventory a company held, the less likely it was to be able to find what it needed. Rather than the American precautionary system of holding huge stocks of parts, Toyota would move to a technique that became justly famous and came to stand for the whole of the new Japanese take on mass

Taiichi Ohno, the inventor of the Toyota Production System, is hailed today as one of the architects of lean production.

production. This was the system that became known as Kanban after the paper chits used to schedule and track stocks and deliveries of parts.

It meant that deliveries would now arrive from suppliers during each day and even on the hour, as the line ran. The parts stock was stripped back ruthlessly to exactly what was needed in that day or that hour, a high-wire balancing act needing as much subtlety in organization as the traditional Fordist system, but more trust and greater interdependence between companies. 'Just in case' became 'Just in Time' – the name that the Kanban system acquired outside Japan.

This has often been described as a 'pull' system, rather than the River Rouge 'push system' of almost unstoppable flow. Ohno's inspiration in America, he recalled, had not been the car plants alone but supermarkets, which impressed him almost as much and where he had been fascinated to see that shelf stocking took place in response to customer purchases. So Ohno's production line would be seen more like a supermarket where the operatives took what they needed to complete a job. It allowed more flexibility, smaller individual runs, and it flagged faulty parts quickly, before thousands had been made. In time it even led to a degree of personalization of the car and to a line that could make a mix of models.

In contrast to the obsessive vertical integration that Ford practised, delegating the production of subcomponents meant that the emerging Japanese car companies had to find – and even nurture – trusted suppliers to make the parts. At first Western commentators saw this as a sign of weakness. To them, Japanese car brands seemed to be mushroom companies, mere assemblers living off a substratum of myriad components manufacturers. Without enormous back shops filled with components they hardly seemed to qualify as manufacturers.

But gradually the appeal of the system became apparent: Japanese companies retained more economic flexibility since they owned much less unfinished stock, and by diffusing production among many suppliers they could also buffer sales glitches. This system reduced the car makers' need for capital and loans and did not shackle them to a huge, and potentially fatal, commitment both to the ongoing employment of an enormous workforce and to pension schemes of commensurate size.

Add to that the bonus that the supplier, not the car maker, now took over the responsibilities for production scheduling and all the management and supervision overheads. Why own a blast furnace or a steel mill, like Ford, or even a gearbox assembly plant, if someone else would run it, find the capital for it, and bring to the business the unique focus that doing one thing superbly well can do? In this system the suppliers were independent businesses and risk-sharers in the whole project. In some ways, the structure of the renewed car industry is a lot like the pre-modern dispersed gun trade of Birmingham, or the clock workshops and garrets of old Clerkenwell.

In retrospect, it is hard to see why the Ford company found it necessary to own so much. These policies had made Ford and General Motors, for example, contractually bound to monolithic labour forces, which always made scaling back in production a contested and expensive strategy.

But what of the Toyota production line itself? In the classical American and European plants, workers had become, in effect, single-task

robots. By the second half of the twentieth century that was beginning
to look like a stupid idea, partly because the auto industry was the
greatest pioneer in the application of automation in assembly tools
and was starting to deploy actual industrial robots. Of course, these
early machines did not have much power of observation and discrim-
ination. By contrast, men and women 'on the track' could make a huge
contribution to quality, but only if they were not too demoralized and
dehumanized by working conditions.

This could be seen, in some ways, as a reversal of the atomization
of tasks pioneered in Detroit – almost a return to some aspects of craft
production – though Toyota would not describe it in such terms, prefer-
ring to call it simply 'the Toyota way'. But the system really meant that
the line worker was now required to actually use his or her own intelligence and judgement. To think, evaluate and to be involved – not simply
to torque a bolt or place a part. Ohno's systems went some way to making
these 'human robots' more multifunctional and more responsible again.
In part, the Toyota way was to give them back some autonomy.

For example, in the traditional car plant, foremen gave instructions,
men on the line worked at their standardized operations, sweepers came
behind them to clean up, and so on for every task. In Toyota foremen
became team-leaders who worked alongside the rest, while the team did
maintenance on their tools and cleaned up their own work stations. The
system also brought profound changes to the hierarchy of the factory.

Ohno pioneered his new system with the press tools that made
sheet metal body parts. The press is a machine the size of a small bus
that has a pair of matching, contoured steel dies that come together to
form a piece of flat steel into different parts of the body. In American
plants the press operators fed in flat sheets of steel, stood back, and
pulled the lever while the press smacked down with a force of many tons
to produce the bonnet, wing, boot or whatever. When the time came
around to change the type of body panel needed, the press tool operators
stood down and a team of specialized tool-setters (higher status and
higher paid) moved in to change the dies. But why, Ohno wondered,
shouldn't the press tool operators make the changes themselves? It would

not have worked in old Detroit, where job demarcations had become ruthlessly entrenched, but in Nagoya the new teams proved they were able to beat the old system hands down, performing tool changes in hours that sometimes took days in old-style plants.

The first wave of cars exported from Japan were often reviled for ungainly styling and rather basic technical features. No one bought a Toyota Corona or a Nissan Bluebird in the 1960s for the comfort of an American sedan or the kind of hairline steering owners of BMWs or Alfa Romeos enjoyed. But gradually the penny dropped that these Japanese cars were fantastically reliable. One other tenet of the new Japan production system was an eagle eye on quality.

Most people are familiar with images of the almost balletic movement of cars, workers and tools as they pass down the assembly line, growing more complete at every stage. But, before the new production philosophy at Toyota (and their other Japanese rivals), manufacturing was seldom as flawless as the industrial theatre of the production line seemed to suggest.

One view that few industrial tourists in the old-style car factories seldom caught, unless glimpsed through an open door, was a line of incomplete or faulty vehicles parked up in a large hall waiting for 're-work' or special attention, although every plant had them. The worker on the line might spot a fault, or a bolt that would not line up, but if he or she could not fix it in the few seconds scheduled for the task as the car slowly jogged by on the conveyor he could flag it with a sticker that meant it was pulled off the track for rectification (individual attention) and parked like a guilty secret – anything, as long as the line did not stop.

To Ohno and the Toyota team this was anathema. Rectification was a sign of failure. It was a sign, for one thing, that quality had failed somewhere in the production chain and it implied that other sin: waste. Waste can be a waste of material, or a waste of time – but it can never be recovered. In the American (read 'world') system of mass production, quality was someone's job – a designated inspector – but not the responsibility of the person on the line. Toyota made it everyone's job.

To emphasize this Ohno brought in a radical new idea. The workers would actually control the line. Any worker, it was declared, could stop the line if they spotted a problem, such as a run of parts coming through that didn't fit properly or anything that prejudiced quality. Better to fix the problem than to build more units of junk. Opinions differ as to how much this statement was rhetorical, and how real. How often did an assembly worker hit the awful button and bring the line to a halt while sirens hooted and lights flashed? We don't know, but when a team from the Massachusetts Institute of Technology published their '5-million-dollar 5-year study on the future of the automobile' in 1990, they claimed that an unnamed German luxury brand, famed for quality, spent more on its rework and rectification department than Toyota did on the whole process of making the cars right the first time.[39]

Toyota, in fact, turned the familiar equation that relates quality to cost upside down. In the West, quality was a premium feature that the customer could be charged more for. In Toyota, quality lapses were seen as a penalty that cost the company a surcharge to fix.

The new ways came to be called 'lean production' and today there are schools of lean production, lean academies and lean gurus. But the American (or the British) car industries had not always been defensive, aggressive, confrontational and narrowly specialized. Back in the 1900s *Engineering Magazine* championed Ford and other production innovators as promoting 'the progressive efficiency movement'. It seems that Henry Ford and his engineers were pretty lean too when their own flow line production techniques were coming of age.

Perhaps every system must become sclerotic with time. Departments multiply, management structures develop that cannot be gainsaid, and structures that were once expedient become permanent and baroque. And so, perhaps, Fordism had to be strained through the filter of another country and another culture in order to re-emerge, even in the land of its birth, as a renewed success.

Perhaps, too, Ohno's vision could only have originally taken root in a culture with a high degree of social cohesion and a high degree of shared purpose, and specifically in Japan where there was a national will for recovery and for regaining prosperity after the Second World War.

And like Ford earlier, Toyota was not secretive about its techniques – in fact, it showed them proudly. For example, when asked at a conference in 1979 why Japanese experts were sharing these secrets internationally, the production engineer Professor Naoto Sasaki allegedly replied, 'You won't do it anyway, and even if you do, it will take ten years to catch up to where we are now and in that time we will be even further ahead.' But he was proved wrong. After convulsions that closed many old-style car plants in the 'first industrial nations', the new Japanese systems did begin to permeate Western car companies, already staggering under the impact of Japanese imports. At first these changes seemed merely, even insultingly, cosmetic.

Battle lines had been drawn between labour and management long ago, and the exhortatory slogans, quality control circles, shared canteens and uniforms and other innovations that European and American managements imported from Japan seemed to be just one more way of getting more work for the same money. Initially the Japanese production ethos proved quite hard to implant in established Western industrial and social structures. British Leyland gradually crumbled, and the Longbridge (Birmingham) plant is no more. Detroit became a ghost town.

Car production, it was clear, had to embrace new techniques, a new style of management, even a new sociology of the car plant if it was to survive in its original host countries. Gradually the Japanese philosophy began to take root around the world, often in all-new factories far from the old automobile centres. In the UK, Nissan chose Sunderland, Honda went to Swindon, and Toyota picked Derbyshire and an engine plant at Deeside in North Wales. All these areas had traditions of engineering and of industry, but no previous role in car production.

In the USA Toyota chose open country at Georgetown, Kentucky, for its new plant, far away from anywhere that had ever built a car before. Today it has turned out 10 million Toyotas the new way and the quality is reckoned to be fully up to Japanese standards.

THE LEAN WORLD

Today these assembly principles have spread far beyond cars. In the high street, Uniqlo, Gap and Primark rely on Fordism brought to tailoring. And according to the British Sandwich Association, Britain consumes 3.5 billion shop-bought sandwiches a year – a trade worth £7.85 billion. Virtually all of these were made on pure flow-line production principles, for otherwise this astonishing volume would be impossible to deliver. Similarly, our laptops, the hard drives inside them, smartphones, and almost all electronic home and business products are made on rigorously organized production lines.

Ford's flow-line factories were remarkable innovations, an extraordinary evolution in industrial life. Inevitably there was scope for improvement and then Toyota developed startling and insightful refinements. But have the principles of Ford's lines and Toyota's new lean production diffused into other cultures so kindly?

In 2010 a number of workers at Foxconn (also known as Hon Hai Precision), a Taiwanese company that also has huge plants in China, committed suicide by jumping from Foxconn buildings. Foxconn, once called 'the biggest company you have never heard of', manufactures electronics under contract – more than 50 per cent, it is claimed, of all the electronics in the world. The company's notorious response was to rig anti-suicide nets around their buildings.

Two years later a group of Foxconn workers threated suicide en masse. To some analysts the promises of 'new' or lean (there is even 'post-lean') mass production have not been borne out in terms of empowerment and more fulfilling employment. It is not only the inventories and the wait times that have been made more lean: it is, critics say, a further extrapolation of Fordism into every worker's day with 'micro-tasks' reducing relief time and wringing unworked seconds from each minute.[40] The *Daily Telegraph* reported that 'workers are reduced to repeating exactly the same hand movements for months on end . . . when they are walking down the street they cannot help but mimic the motion.'[41] Perhaps, in a way, the plight of these newly regimented workers recalls the earlier strain in Europe when the comparatively free weavers and craftsmen of the emerging industrial era were forced out of their homes or informal workshops into systematized factories run on a new time – that of the steam engine, or the clock.

The association of Foxconn with Apple ensured that these events would be a continuing global news story. (Foxconn, for example, makes Acer and Dell computers too.) It is hard, though, to reach a statistically informed view about the incidence of suicide there. It requires comparisons with the general suicide rate in China (in itself disputed) and calibration against other industries and other economies undergoing intense social and economic change. One commentator suggests that the rate is actually higher among American college students in a similar age group. But the reportage reflects the great unease in the affluent world about this extraordinary and recent global arrangement whereby so much consumption is supported by distant manufacture. When the jobs were moved offshore, did we also export political oversight and moral responsibility? Recently, however, Foxconn unveiled a plan to invest some $3 billion in a new factory and display screen plant in south Wisconsin and to generate a huge economic boost to the area. If it happens there will be another way to assess the new Chinese interpretation of post-Ford production-line working, although recent reports imply that the project seems stalled and the 13,000 jobs promised might not materialize.[42]

Lean production has certainly become a movement, with lean institutes and academic courses. But there are many economies, and many products, where 'lean' just means tough. As global production has become so prevalent, and container ship transport so cheap, it sometimes seems that competitive advantage in industrial production comes down to national systems of authority and the degree of autonomy and political expression that workers possess. The congeniality of production-line living, it seems, may depend on where you are lucky enough to live as much as on the detail of the production system.

In Crewe, or Oxford, or in Kentucky, workers build Bentleys, Minis and Toyotas and modern lean production seems to bring a lifestyle that

Ferrari production today. Naturally, Ferrari production is special, but now even budget cars are made in spotless facilities very unlike the first flow lines.

many workers find genuinely congenial. There are often coffee break areas with ferns or palms, magazines and books. At Maranello, Ferrari employees work in a spotless environment with palpable pride. Their equipment is the finest and the buildings on the Ferrari campus are designed by a selection of Italy's most esteemed architects (the wind tunnel is the work of Renzo Piano).

But all these are premium products. In other markets, in producer countries where margins are tighter and social underpinnings are scanty, perhaps lean can just mean tough.

'THE PARTS ARE MEN'

The production line ultimately realized the project for systematic rational manufacture that the Enlightenment started back in the eighteenth century. Later, intriguingly, Ford and his methods impressed both Hitler and Lenin. For his own part, Ford even claimed to have rewritten the laws of economics by lowering the cost of production and creating a more affluent industrial class that could, in effect, afford its own products. The Ford prosperity recipe, he crowed, was high wages, low prices, and mass production.

The historian Simon Schaffer has argued convincingly that one of the lesser understood ambitions of Enlightenment thinking was 'to turn men into machines', to extract the knowledge of the secretive craftsman and put the workplace under the direction of 'a philosopher'.[43] Writing in the eighteenth century, the Scottish Enlightenment historian and philosopher Adam Ferguson put this explicitly, arguing that 'many mechanical arts, indeed, require no capacity; they succeed best under a total suppression of sentiment and reason . . . Manufactures, accordingly, prosper most where the mind is least consulted and where the workshop may . . . be considered as an engine, the parts of which are men.'[44]

This could be a perfect description of Ford's Highland Park factory in the 1920s, or of an electronics factory in China today.

3

THE GODFATHER OF OIL

'How is it possible to capture the sweet and carefree atmosphere of 1913, and 1914 until the outbreak of the First World War? Never had Europe been so prosperous and gay. Never had the world gone so well for all classes of the community: especially in England.'[1] Alongside the London society of this charmed belle époque that Osbert Sitwell described in his exotic memoir *Great Morning* lay another world in which a new technological arms race was being played out alongside grim technological and diplomatic calculations.

Beyond Britain's shores ranged the Royal Navy, the greatest unified military instrument ever seen and, for much of its existence, the largest single integrated industrial and technological enterprise in the world. But though the Pax Britannica it secured may have seemed eternal in the Edwardian world, the German wish, or particularly the will of Kaiser Wilhelm II, to possess a new and substantial fleet brought an unwelcome and threatening element.

To British politicians and diplomats, the German programme to build battleships seemed to be a new and threatening kind of destabilizing brinkmanship and the start of a dangerous arms race that would actually add to Germany's dangers and to the instability of Europe. Few in Britain could fathom or empathize with the German sense of disentitlement and resentment – or perhaps of insecurity – and though Germany argued that the new fleet was required to protect its colonies, its trade and its expanding world interests, naval analysts concluded that the character and short range of its new ships seemed to suit them really to the North Sea, where the only foe was the Royal Navy.

Why should a new state with no naval tradition be so avid to possess a fearsome fleet? It could never, in fact, match the Royal Navy in numbers and power, and British politicians said explicitly that the popular will to have and to pay for a supremely powerful Royal Navy was solid. Britain would outbuild potential enemies in Dreadnoughts. Nonetheless, the new German navy was a worrying upset to calculations of deterrence and immunity. It was, hazarded Winston Churchill in a political speech in Glasgow in 1912, a 'luxury fleet'. He declaimed that

> The purposes of British naval power are essentially defensive. We have no thoughts . . . of aggression . . . The British Navy to us is a necessity . . . the German Navy is to them more in the nature of a luxury . . . Whatever is needed [in shipbuilding] for the safety of the country will be asked for by the Government.[2]

The speech caused great offence in Germany and the fleet building continued. It was, to a great extent, the pet project of Wilhelm II, who, in a later assessment, Churchill described as 'a very ordinary, vain, but, on the whole well-meaning man, hoping to pass himself off as a second Frederick the Great [but who had] no long policy of cautious statecraft, no calculation, no deep insight'.[3]

The naval competition that ensued led to bigger guns (the greatest yet forged in Britain), greater ships, new engines giving more speed and power, and in consequence a move to oil fuel, rather than coal as before. It also led inevitably to a new geopolitical venture – deep British involvement in the Near and Middle East to ensure the continued supply of the navy's essential fuel. This included a major role in the definition and government of the Arab states that were established following the First World War – an ongoing strategic involvement driven by oil – as well as Britain's ambivalent posture during the years of its responsibility for Palestine and its actions after the Second World War during the emergence of the state of Israel.

THE 'DEMONIC' FISHER

The British navy had been unchallenged since the Battle of Trafalgar
a century before. The effect of this new threat was to inspire it to revolutionize and reform itself at an extraordinary rate. The main agent
of change was Jacky Fisher, the extraordinary, devious, ingenious and
opinionated Admiral of the Fleet, scrapping obsolete ships, laying off
time-worn officers and grasping at technical innovation in engines,
guns and armour.

It was a process that was carried out with astonishing acrimony.
Fisher was an elemental, some said 'demonic' figure, obsessively committed to his own vision. His 1929 autobiographical memoir, read today,
seems almost unhinged, but gives a glimpse of the man and his mission.

> And so, to-day, I will begin this book – not an autobiography, but
> a collection of memories of a lifelong war against limpets, parasites,
> sycophants, and jellyfish . . . At times they stung; but that only
> made me more relentless, ruthless and remorseless.[4]
>
> . . . All the old women of both sexes . . . squirmed when I did
> away with 19½ millions sterling of parasites in ships, officers and
> men, between 1904 and 1910! They squirmed when, at one big
> plunge, we introduced the Turbine in the Dreadnought (the Turbine
> only before having been in a penny steamboat). They squirmed at
> my introduction of the water tube Boiler, when I put the fire where
> the water used to be and the water where the fire used to be! . . .
> They squirmed when I concentrated 88 per cent of the British Fleet
> in the North Sea.[5]

Fisher's reform programme (or perhaps it was partly Fisher himself)
was vehemently resisted by some officers and particularly by Sir Charles
Beresford, latterly Admiral of the Channel Fleet. For a while it amounted
to a virtual civil war within the navy (Fisher's supporters called it a
'mutiny'), which a weak Cabinet allowed to fester. There were Beresford
men and there were Fisher men. For example, among those in the 'Fish

Churchill and Lord Fisher leaving a meeting of the Committee of Imperial Defence, 1913.

Winston Churchill at the launch of the battleship HMS *Centurion* at Devonport in 1911. Lord Fisher is to the left.

pond' was the gunnery expert Percy Scott, who reformed the way guns were aimed and ranged and who emphasized the importance of gunnery practice at a time when the navy was quite casual about gunnery and satisfied with unrealistic firing tests. Scott drove through a series of improvements and was an avid proponent of systematic target practice. However, the greatest innovation lay in the introduction of 'director firing', which meant transferring the job of aiming the guns away from individual crews in the gun turrets to a controlling gunnery officer, high up in an observation post on a mast above the smoke of guns and boilers, and equipped with telescopic range-finding gear. Crucially, this gunnery control station was also equipped with a 'fire control director', a complex mechanical proto-computer designed by the naval officer Frederic Charles

Dreyer.[6] Today the machine looks like some steampunk cyber-fantasy, but it took inputs including the ship speed, its compass heading, wind speed, the range of the target and estimates of the target's heading and speed, to calculate a firing solution that was passed to all the guns. Of course, the directing gunnery officer would also spot the fall of the salvoes and could enter a manual correction.

Jacky Fisher in 1917. His extraordinary face and manner, puck-like, threatening or charming, inspired Jan Morris to write a short study of the man simply entitled 'Fisher's Face'.

Like Fisher, Scott tended to express himself with remarkable fearlessness and ferocity. Ordered into harbour during training manoeuvres in 1907 by his commander, Admiral Sir Charles Beresford, to prepare the ships for a State visit of the German emperor, Scott invited court martial by signalling openly to his squadron that 'paintwork seems to be more in demand than gunnery so you had better come in to make yourself look pretty by the 8th.' This earned the fury of Beresford, who demanded Scott's dismissal from command of the First Cruiser Squadron as being 'contemptuous in tone, insubordinate in character

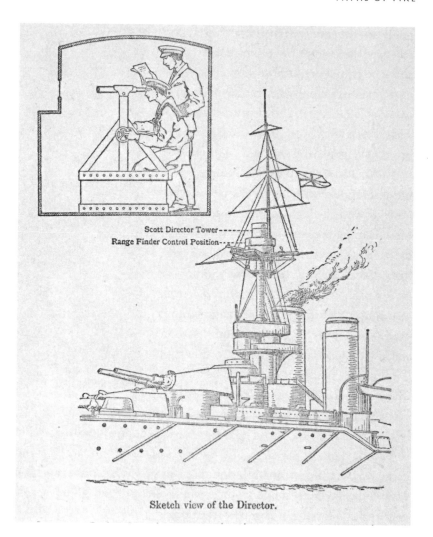

Scott Director Tower
Range Finder Control Position

Sketch view of the Director.

Principles of director firing, from Admiral Sir Percy Scott, *Fifty Years in the Royal Navy* (1919).

and wanting in dignity'.[7] Perhaps only the power of ridicule saved him. In Parliament, Captain Arthur Murray, MP for Kincardineshire, referring clearly to Beresford, called the Channel paint affair 'a sickening tale of effeminate sensitiveness and huff', while a cabaret jingle started circulating London in Service clubs and Mayfair society haunts:

Oh Percy Scott, it's tommy rot for you to go on firing
While I grow faint for want of paint we ought to be admiring,

Your guns are good and once they stood a pledge for England's
honour.

But now it's fits, 'Donner und Blitz' to paint a real Madonna.
Dear Percy Scott, I've really not quite wholly lost my temper,
So take your ships, get on the slips and daub them with
distemper!

Admiral Sir Percy Scott
in ceremonial regalia,
frontispiece to *Fifty Years
in the Royal Navy* (1919).

THE NEW NAVY

This revolution in British gunnery, armour and machinery was signalled dramatically in 1906 by the launching of the new battleship HMS
Dreadnought. It had more gun power, more speed and more armour
plate than any ship in the world.

In spite of his hyperbole, these innovations were not solely the
product of Fisher's genius, though of course he was intensely interested
in invention and modernization. Throughout the late 1800s firms like
Sir William Armstrong on Tyneside and Krupp in Essen had been
experimenting with steels and with armour. Pages of *The Engineer* from
that epoch show terrifying images of comparative trials of armour plate
of different thickness and composition, tested by projectiles fired from
enormous naval guns. Some show resistance, blistered and pockmarked;
some are hideously bulged; some smashed through. Although this is
dispassionate engineering science and cutting-edge metallurgy, it is
impossible to forget, seeing these images, that one day there will be
men on the other side of that plating.

Meanwhile, guns were growing in size and strength, increasing
the charge they could stand, their range and the weight of shell they
could throw. But perhaps the greatest transformation was the turbine
power plant. The steam piston engines fitted at the end of the nineteenth
century were vast affairs, perhaps 6 m (20 ft) high and even longer. A
battleship would have at least two of these, together generating 8,000–
10,000 horsepower and fed by multiple boilers, distributed around the
ship to make it less vulnerable to incapacitating shell strikes. There was
no easy way to find more power, short of adding engines, or making

them larger, but the interior of a battleship was already a miracle of packaging that juggled coal bunkers, crew quarters and magazines for the ammunition. There was no space to be won without giving something up.

Up on Tyneside, however, was the remarkable inventor Charles Parsons. He was an engineer (educated as a premium apprentice at Sir William Armstrong's works), a mathematician (Dublin and Cambridge) and an industrialist on his own account. He was also, unusually for an engineer back then, from a titled family, being the youngest son of William Parsons, 3rd Earl of Rosse, the eminent astronomer whose many discoveries included the Whirlpool (spiral) galaxy (M51), using enormous telescopes he had specified and built at Birr Castle in Ireland.

After various engineering jobs, Charles conceived a passion to develop the steam turbine, then a mechanical novelty. The conventional steam piston engine – vast, durable and stately – was virtually at the end of its development. It was complex, almost baroque, with numerous supplementary pumps, devices and accessories to sustain it and improve

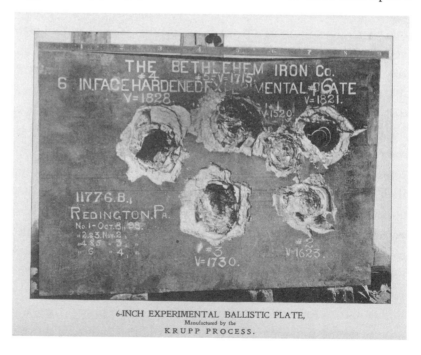

Effects of shot on a compound armour plate.

6-INCH EXPERIMENTAL BALLISTIC PLATE,
Manufactured by the
KRUPP PROCESS.

Rolling armour plates at the Atlas works, Sheffield, from the *Illustrated London News*, 14 September 1861.

its efficiency, and it could not give more power without growing in size, which, we have noted, was unacceptable. If it could spin faster, that would help, but at a stately 95 revolutions a minute, the normal top speed, the forces from the massive pistons, which reversed direction at every stroke, were at the maximum the engine structure could stand.

The Parsons turbine, by contrast, was a pure rotary machine.[8] The sole moving part was the main rotor, a series of discs, each carrying a ring of vanes – little winglets – through which the steam flowed, giving each one a constant push. The turbine was free of vibration, could spin at unprecedented speeds, generate ample power and was extremely compact. Parsons's machines quickly transformed electricity generation and he then turned to marine propulsion, building the 32-metre (105 ft) steam launch *Turbinia* powered by his new engine, which was worked up to speed over a measured mile on the Tyne.

In June 1897 a review of the Royal Navy was held at Spithead, in the Solent, ostensibly to celebrate Queen Victoria's Diamond Jubilee – sixty years of her rule. It was a vast affair, with fifty battleships and 170 naval vessels in all formed up in two parallel lines, 11 km (7 mi.) long. Then *Turbinia*, apparently a gatecrasher to the grand event, began a high-speed run between the assembled lines. In timed trials later, she proved capable of 34.5 knots (almost 40 mph). What speed she was doing on that day is not known but it was probably some 30 knots, about 10 knots more than the fastest vessels in the navy. Unfortunately, one naval patrol boat officiously attempted to cross her path to head her off, although it badly underestimated her speed. *Turbinia*, piloted by Christopher Leyland, a director of the Parsons company, just managed to steer behind her, narrowly escaping a collision that seemed so close that the naval lieutenant in command could be seen unbuckling his heavy ceremonial sword, expecting to have to swim for his life.

Leyland recalled that, as they crossed, 'he evidently spoke to me, and I said something to him, but as we were passing at nearly 45 knots, it may have been just as well that our impromptu remarks did not carry.' Piloting the *Turbinia* that day, Leyland remembered, 'was almost too exciting'.[9]

Many believed at the time that *Turbinia*'s appearance was an impertinent and irresponsible publicity stunt. But Leyland was actually a well-connected former Royal Navy officer and had commanded a gunboat. The general view is that technically progressive officers in the

William Orpen, *Sir Charles Algernon Parsons*, c. 1905–10, oil on canvas.

Royal Navy, perhaps with impetus from Fisher, had quietly asked Leyland and Parsons to demonstrate the potential of the steam turbine ship that day and to help persuade the Admiralty to adopt it for the next generation of warships.

One aim for the Spithead review, no doubt, had been to discourage German naval expansionism, and Prince Henry of Prussia, the brother of Kaiser Wilhelm II, was in attendance to represent him. Surely the long, sombre lines of battleships, signifying immense power (and expense), would deter a naval arms race? This clearly did not work. German naval expansion continued, but the turbine demonstration did mark a shift in British policy. When HMS *Dreadnought* was launched in 1906, its strikingly high speed was achieved with Parsons turbine power plants.

Photograph of the *Turbinia* taken during one of the test runs, c. 1897. She is travelling at a speed of over 30 knots, and the passengers have to hold on to the guard rails.

Turbinia on a high-speed run, 1894. The figure in the bridge is thought to be Parsons's partner Christopher Leyland. Charles Parsons was usually out of sight supervising the engine controls.

WINSTON CHURCHILL AND FISHER'S RETURN

When appointed as First Lord of the Admiralty in 1911 Winston Churchill surveyed the progress of modernization of the Royal Navy and on Fisher's role in command of it in the years leading up to the First World War. Churchill reflected that Fisher 'shook . . . every department of the Navy . . . and beat them and cajoled them out of slumber into intense activity . . . the Navy was not a pleasant place while this was going on,' and, he mused, 'could we not have had the Fisher reforms without the Fisher methods?'

Nevertheless, Churchill quickly sent for Fisher, now seventy years old and in retirement, arguing that 'his genius was deep and true . . . the originality of his mind and the spontaneity of his nature freed him from conventionalities of all kinds,' although he marvelled that:

> For a man who for so many years filled great official positions and was charged with so much secret and deadly business, Lord Fisher appeared amazingly voluminous and reckless in his correspondence . . . [His letters] were dashed off red-hot as they left his mind, his strong pen galloping along in the wake of the imperious thought. He would often audaciously fling out on paper thoughts which other people would hardly admit to their own minds. It is small wonder that his turbulent passage left so many foes foaming in his wake. The wonder is that he did not shipwreck himself a score of times. The buoyancy of his genius alone supported the burden. Indeed, in the process of years the profuse and imprudent violence of his letters became, in a sense, its own protection. People came to believe that this was the breezy style appropriate to our guardians of the deep, and the old Admiral swept forward on his stormy course.[10]

Churchill had originally been an 'economizer' in Parliament, supporting the social programmes that the Liberal government was introducing. But through European events, and particularly through German arms expenditure, Churchill came to see his task as to build ships and maintain the supremacy of the navy. The *Dreadnought* of 1906 had been a striking step, but it was only the beginning. New, faster and more heavily armed ships had to follow. Churchill claimed that the three programmes of 1912, 1913 and 1914 comprised the greatest additions in power and cost ever made to the navy. It was, in every sense, an 'arms race', before that term was current. But even as the designs were being finalized, the possibility arose of equipping the next generation of, then partly built, British battleships with new 15-inch guns, bigger than any yet built and throwing a shell weighing nearly a ton. Churchill recalled that 'in one of those nightmare novels that used to appear from time to time before the war, I read . . . of a great battle in which, to the amazement of the defeated British Fleet, the German new vessels opened fire with a terrible, unheard-of 15-inch gun.'[11]

Churchill, almost as impetuous at times as Fisher, was deeply excited by the prospect of the 15-inch gun, throwing a shell nearly half as heavy again as the biggest fired by the German fleet:

> Enlarging the gun meant enlarging the ships, and enlarging the ships meant increasing the cost. Moreover, the redesign must cause no delay and the guns must be ready as soon as the turrets were ready. No such thing as a modern 15-inch gun existed . . . Armstrongs were consulted in deadly secrecy and they undertook to execute it . . . We knew the 13.5-inch gun well . . . All sorts of new stresses might develop in the 15-inch model . . . If only we could make a trial gun and test it thoroughly before giving the orders for the whole of the guns of all of the five ships, there would be no risk; but then we should lose an entire year, and five great vessels would go into the line of battle carrying an inferior weapon to that which we had it in our power to give them.[12]

And now the steam turbine had demonstrated the possibility of almost doubling the power and gaining a striking jump in speed, from 20 knots to 25 or more, and it seemed imperative that the new ships should have both the new big guns and the more capable turbine, although more powerful engines needed more steam, more boilers and a faster rate of stoking. Only oil fuel offered the possibility of achieving this next new leap in battleship design. Though Britain ran on coal, and indeed coal energy had created its industrial and imperial wealth in the first place, a coal-fired warship was a demanding piece of equipment. Churchill observed that in the battlecruiser *Lion* 'nearly a hundred men were continually occupied . . . shovelling coal from one steel chamber to another without ever seeing the light either of day or of the furnace fires', while 'as a coal ship used up her coal, increasingly large numbers of men had to be taken, if necessary, from the guns to shovel the coal from remote and inconvenient bunkers to bunkers nearer the furnaces.'[13]

Britain, recalled Churchill, had the finest supply of steam coal in the world, 'safe in our mines, under our own hand', and although the change from British coal to foreign oil was 'a formidable decision in itself', he sided with the modernizers because 'Oil gave ships a large excess of speed over coal. It enabled that speed to be attained with far greater rapidity. It gave forty per cent greater radius of action for the same weight of coal.' Oil was easier to stow, easier to deliver to the boiler furnaces by pumps, and faster to heat up the furnaces when high power was demanded.

THE FLEET AND THE FAST SECTION

In 1910 perhaps only the Royal Navy (really, the British state) could afford to bankroll the infrastructure for pumping, bunkering and transporting vast quantities of oil. But the will to make and deploy the ships and the guns unlocked enormous capital resources and huge 'first move' investments that would never be made on rational business grounds.

Churchill set Fisher to preside over a Royal Commission on the supply of oil with the Governor of the Bank of England and the directors of the Anglo-Persian and Burmah oil companies. Oil executives and naval personnel were sent to the Persian Gulf to study the oil fields: 'All through 1912 and 1913 our efforts were unceasing.'

In spite of all this complex statecraft, Fisher took personal credit for the change, crowing that 'Sir Marcus Samuel writes [to *The Times*] that I am the God-father of Oil – and Oil is going to be the fuel of the world.' Churchill, more conscious of the broader flow of history, described the events as narrative:

> From the original desire to enlarge the gun we were led on step by step to the Fast Division, and in order to get the Fast Division we were forced to rely . . . upon oil fuel . . . This led to enormous expense and tremendous opposition . . . Yet it was absolutely impossible to turn back. We could only fight our way forward, and finally, we found our way to the Anglo-Persian Oil agreement.

In Churchill's mind each link in the chain 'had forged the next'.[14]

ORDE WINGATE AND THE PIPELINE

As an easily transported, highly calorific source both of fuel and precious chemicals, oil was bound to find its place in the global economy. America and other powers were discovering the enormous utility of oil and inevitably were also becoming caught up in vast strategic designs in the Middle East.

The UK would also have become increasingly automobilized, though whether it would have become so deeply involved in the detailed arrangements for structure and demarcation of the nations of the Middle East, following the destruction of the Ottoman empire after the First World War, is open to question. And without the navy's thirst for oil, would the UK by the 1930s have had the Anglo-Iraq oil pipeline to defend against attacks by Arab groups incensed by increasing Jewish immigration into Palestine permitted under the British rule (the 'Mandate')? By chance, the local military commander Orde Wingate, tasked with defending the pipeline, was prepared to take the contentious step of arming and training the semi-secret Jewish fighting force, the Haganah, to form 'Special Night Squads' that patrolled, fought and ambushed raiders under his command. It was to form the nucleus for the future Israeli army.

However, it is important to note that Wingate was not playing out a grand British imperial design by arming and training the emerging defence force of what was to become Israel. His motives were personal, unusual and many British officials at the time disapproved. For example, his superior, General Wavell, General Officer Commanding (GOC) British Forces in Palestine and Trans-Jordan, was explicitly opposed to Zionism, considering that it would 'focus antagonism to Britain throughout the region . . . since it was the one subject on which all Arabs were united'. After 1939 he added, 'every acceptance of Jewish offers to help in the war effort would jab and inflame Arab resentment.'[15]

Wingate, nevertheless, succeeded in quietly establishing the special squads, in part because he saw them as the only way to meet his own local military objectives and to achieve enough military force for his task. But Wingate, in complete contradiction to Wavell and to many other British officials, also had a personal mission to assist and support Zionism derived from a devout Christian upbringing in the Plymouth Brethren. The literal interpretation of the Bible that he had imbibed made him a committed believer in Zionism and a supporter of the Jewish desire for a return to Palestine.

A highly unusual man (Lord Moran, Churchill's doctor, described him as 'hardly sane'), Wingate was said to sometimes hold staff meetings stark naked, and also to carry a raw onion on a string round his neck, from which he took fortifying bites through the day. He later went on to train and inspire the Chindits, an elite force trained to achieve deep penetration against the Japanese army in the Burmese jungle.

Members of the Special Night Squads saw the experience with Wingate as a vital component in the creation of the Israeli army, which came into being formally as the Second World War ended. Perhaps without this military experience the new state of Israel would not have survived the war of 1947, possibly the most crucial challenge that the new state has so far encountered.

Wingate's influence and instruction went deep. Moshe Dayan, perhaps Israel's most charismatic general, saw him as a leader who 'taught us everything we know'.[16] Yigael Yadin, a key figure in the Haganah, said of Wingate, 'His basic contribution – and it was a great one – was to teach us that warfare is a science and an art at the same time. He was the perfect example of the military man, being himself the excellent combination of scientist and artist.'[17] Today Wingate is honoured in Israel as 'The Friend' (*Hayedid*). Some think he even dreamed of himself as a new Gideon, leading a new Jewish state to independence at the head of a Jewish army.

JUTLAND AND THE BLOCKADES

Orde Wingate in Burma, 1943.

In the event, did the naval war repay all the inventiveness, talent and treasure that had been expended on the British fleet? In the early stages there were various medium-scale engagements, largely satisfactory to Britain. There was an audacious sally into the German home waters of the Heligoland Bight and an engagement off Dogger Bank. These seemed to show that the British battlecruisers were more than a match for their German equivalents, while the German navy made various jabs, bombarding coastal towns to tempt out British forces. The great fleet battle, however, seemed unlikely until, on 30 May 1916, the Admiralty picked up signals that the German fleet under a new and aggressive commander, Admiral Scheer, was putting to sea. And so too, therefore, did the Royal Navy's Grand Fleet commanded by Sir John Jellicoe.

Thousands of words have been written about the battle that ensued on the following day and it can only be summarized here. The struggle fell into two parts: a battlecruiser engagement at 3.50 p.m. when the scouting forces from both sides met some 130 km (80 mi.) west of Jutland, followed by engagements between the main fleets. The battle-cruiser force commanded by Admiral Beatty, onboard HMS *Lion*, made the first contact at about 3.00 p.m. and he quickly led his battlecruisers against those of Franz von Hipper. The gunnery contest turned against the British, however, even though Beatty had six cruisers to Hipper's five. The German cruiser gunnery was, it seems, altogether more accurate.[18] Moreover, as the engagement began, Beatty had failed to fire at long range even though his bigger guns outdistanced Hipper's. Instead he closed the distance, giving away the advantage that all the technological enthusiasm of Fisher, Churchill and Percy Scott had brought to his big guns and bringing his force within reach of Hipper's armament, which quickly demonstrated that it was aimed and directed more keenly. Two of Beatty's cruisers were struck at a range of about 14,000 yards (8 land mi.) and blew clear apart, probably because plunging shells (arcing down because of the long range) penetrated the decks, ignited the magazines and exploded the cordite stored below for the guns. This is the point at which Beatty is said to have remarked, 'there seems to be something wrong with our bloody ships today. Steer two points [closer to the enemy].'[19]

For reasons that have never been fully resolved, in his move to engage Hipper, Beatty had left behind part of his scouting force, the four, much stronger *Queen Elizabeth*-class battleships commanded by Admiral Evan-Thomas. But now Evan-Thomas's battleships began to catch up and, firing at the extraordinary distance of 16 km (10 mi.), began to damage Hipper's ships and almost certainly saved the rest of the cruiser squadron. These were the ships of the famous Fast Division that Fisher, Churchill and the naval constructors had laboured so hard to provide. From the British point of view, it was a tragedy that the cruisers and the fast battleships had not attacked as a unified force.

Beatty then began the 'run to the North' intended to draw Hipper (and the main German fleet he was presumed to be screening) up to Jellicoe and the Grand Fleet. From about 6.25 p.m., the main fleets did meet, and British fire, now displaying remarkable accuracy, started to strike the German ships. At this point Scheer, fearing he was about to be enveloped by the whole British fleet, then turned his ships and escaped westwards. But curiously, after some minutes steaming west, he reversed direction and returned back towards the east. Perhaps, as he later wrote, he sought to renew the battle, or perhaps he had wrongly estimated the arrangement of the British fleet and hoped to pass 'under its tail' and lead his ships to home port. As it turned out, he sailed straight into the centre of Jellicoe's fleet, which unleashed the heaviest cannonade ever fired at sea. From the German perspective, the whole eastern horizon was a flickering sheet of flame from the British guns.

In the light of later controversy about director firing and the quality of British equipment, it is noticeable that Admiral Hipper reflected that

The fire of . . . the bulk of the enemy, produced an excellent impression. The salvoes arrived absolutely dense (with no spread). The fall in elevation and direction covered almost the same spot. The firing constituted a proof of the care with which the British have eliminated in their guns all influences which increase the 'spread,' and of the most remarkable manner in which the English

Admiral Beatty's flagship *Lion* (behind a shell-burst in the water), and beside *Queen Mary*, blowing up, Jutland, 1916.

fire control arrangements have been produced, both [in] elevation and direction.[20]

The light was fading and Jellicoe declined to follow the retreating battleships into the dark for fear of torpedoes and mines.

Perhaps battle would be renewed at first light, but by an extraordinary combination of boldness and luck, Scheer turned eastward in the dark and slipped through the British forces, returning to Wilhelmshaven as dawn broke.

Following the battle, Germany immediately claimed a great victory. British news management was slow and maladroit, wasting much time before affirming a counterclaim. Many were disappointed that the German fleet had not been convincingly smashed, but the Admiralty had actually approved Jellicoe's cautious policies in advance. Even Churchill conceded that Jellicoe had been the one man who could lose the war in an afternoon. He had not lost: he had preserved a naval force that was still overwhelmingly superior.

Although it is also true that these terrifying fleets were, in effect, hostage to each other, spending most of the war locked up in their

Aftermath: HMS *Barham* in port, shell damage, June 1916.

Aftermath: SMS *Seydlitz* in harbour after the battle, 6 June 1916.

secure home bases of Kiel and Scapa Flow, the United Kingdom still held undisputed command of the oceans after Jutland. Until submarine war started in earnest in 1917 Allied ships sailed freely around the world and even announced their dates of departure. The insurance rate for commercial shipping was just 1 per cent. Allied ships also transported some 20 million men around the theatres of war and across the Channel.

In the light of engagements like Jutland, one historian has argued convincingly for 'the failure of the heavy gun at sea', pointing out the low percentage of hits and the enormous expenditure of shells to destroy an enemy ship.[21] But does that matter? The same accusation of wastage could also apply to machine guns. From a technological point of view, perhaps the chief problem with these awesome warships was that gunnery, engines and armour were at a high pitch but they had run far ahead of command and control techniques. One of Jellicoe's urgent and futile signals to Beatty on the afternoon of 31 May was: 'Where is the enemy's main battle fleet?' Neither side, in fact, knew. Some communication was by primitive and patchy radio links, but mostly it was by masthead semaphores and signal flags. Speeds and gun

HMS *Iron Duke* leading a long line of warships, July 1914.

striking range had risen so much that ships were often widely spaced and these signals were displayed at the utmost limits of visibility. In retrospect it seems that the technology of warships had developed in an unbalanced way and that these new ships, firing at long range and capable of unprecedented speed, had really outrun the techniques of communication and control that had served navies well until then.

Nevertheless, the main objective of pre-war policy for the use of British naval power was, in effect, successful. The aim was to ensure free oceanic trade for itself and its allies and completely inhibit it among its enemies. Although no great engagement occurred which extinguished the German fleet, British naval power secured free trade for Britain, France and their allies across all the oceans of the world and the Allies transported millions of troops by sea, while the British blockade of Germany at sea was almost absolute: almost no German commercial traffic of any kind sailed, except in the Baltic and along the Dutch coast, leaving Sweden as the major maritime trading partner.

German economic life and well-being was clearly being squeezed and this certainly contributed to the end.

Admiral Percy Scott had a pithy view on the Battle of Jutland, opining in *The Times* that Jellicoe had fought the battle he planned to fight. Commenting on the actions later in the afternoon, he suggested that in the main fleet action the Grand Fleet battleships made more than seventy hits on the German ships 'and received in return just two shells and one torpedo. 70–3 is a walkover by any standards . . . Whatever Jellicoe did, the Germans came out for the battle of Jutland and they all went home and never came out again, except to surrender.'

In fact, if the losses sustained by Beatty's cruiser squadron earlier in the day are subtracted from the British side, the total losses of ships, and of men, are remarkably similar. In any event, the damage suffered by the enormous British fleet was very far from weakening it enough to allow Scheer to risk another engagement. In 1918, however, as Ludendorff's land offensive in the west was failing, Admiral Scheer did propose that the fleet sail out to try and dent British sea power in order, it seems, to obtain better peace terms from its enemies. Perhaps Jutland did ultimately prove a victory for the British government, although a slow-burning one, for German sailors considered this next proposed battle a 'death ride'. Three hundred crew disappeared ashore overnight, and in the following days mutinies spread round the fleet. The threat of another sea battle was the seed of the whole sequence of disorder, rebellion and political collapse that spread through Germany, carried by deputations of disaffected sailors to all the big cities. Shortly afterwards, the Kaiser abdicated and fled for asylum in the Netherlands. The mutiny in his cherished fleet was the trigger that brought the end.

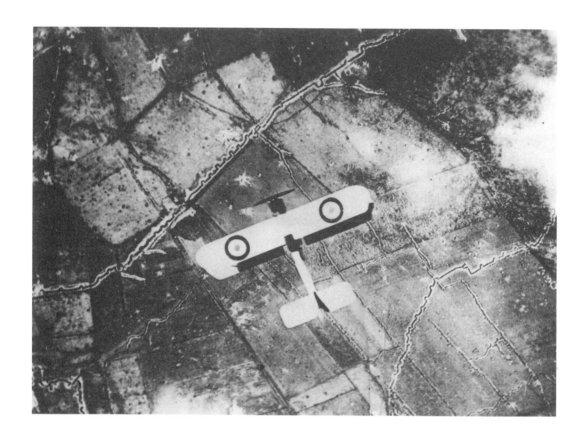

The frighteningly
revealing power of
aerial photography
was a major stimulus
for anti-aircraft
gunnery. Trench lines
and fortifications are
clearly visible. A Royal
Flying Corps BE.2C
reconnaissance aircraft
in flight over the
Western Front, 1916.

4

HIGH PHEASANTS IN
THEORY AND PRACTICE

If you had been invited to a Berkshire estate sometime in the 1920s
you might have encountered an extraordinary spectacle. A small Ford
Model T truck was jolting urgently along an estate road, engine strain-
ing at the limits of its power. One side of the vehicle was completely
obscured by a whitewashed steel sheet fixed to it from end to end. Off
to one side, about 40 yards away in the grass, stood Major Sir Gerald
Burrard, stoutly clad in his tweed shooting gear, boots and breeches,
with a favoured 12 bore Purdey at the ready. As the Ford came level,
the Major shouldered the shotgun and, swinging along its track, fired
squarely onto the whitewashed plate.

The shot struck the plate with a resounding crash, which must have
sounded appalling to the driver on the other side of it, but in fact he
was in little danger. After each shot the driver pulled up and the Major
hurried over to inspect the pattern on the plate, for he was trying to
resolve an ancient mystery. Did firing at a moving target somehow dilute
the pattern of pellets and reduce its effectiveness? Tests went well, only
handicapped by the extreme difficulty of getting the elderly Ford up
to 40 mph, a speed that the Major considered would be representative
of a game bird going well downwind.[1]

Trying shotguns against whitewashed steel plates at various ranges
was a well-established way of testing them. A good 'pattern' spread a
circle of shot evenly, leaving no bunches or empty holes that a bird
might fly through. But these plates for gunsmiths' trials were fixed to
the ground. Burrard's notion was that the charge of shot did not arrive

Both sides of the Model T truck used by Major Sir Gerald Burrard for his moving target ballistics experiments.

all at once and so probably the static plate did not indicate the true effectiveness of the gun against a real, moving target.

In addition, it had been known for many years that to shoot a bird on the wing, it was necessary to swing the gun along its line of flight, overtaking it to 'lead' the target. The shot, it was clear, had to be aimed ahead at where the bird was shortly going to be. Some shooters thought that the very act of swinging the gun would tend to spread out the shot pattern along the flight path, as if it were a garden hose, but Burrard disposed of that idea with some brisk mathematics.

What interested him most was that the pellets did not all arrive at once because they came out of the barrel as a column which then became a cloud with appreciable width but also spread out in depth along the line of flight, so that the pellets arrived at different times. If the target was stationary the effect was irrelevant, but if it was moving, what then? The shot pattern was presumably more open and the quarry might fly through the holes and be on its way before the tail of cloud came through. So, were the gunmakers' regular patterns that they proudly displayed to customers actually achieved in the field or, in reality, were they distorted and 'strung out' when fired at a fast-crossing target? Hence the Ford truck and the firing experiments. The bullseye on the side of the Ford truck represented a notional crossing pheasant, and at 40 mph it covered 6 feet in one-tenth of a second.[2] His conclusion was that the pattern effectiveness was actually diminished by up to 10 per cent, depending on the angle of the shot, although later writers have tended to consider that this dilution is not decisive.

Burrard had been a professional artilleryman, so what was more natural than to use his army expertise in retirement to make his favourite sport more rational and less superstitious? He also served as an expert witness in firearms cases and, in what he described in Sherlockian terms as 'the case of the shot Cypriot doctor', helped to free a pastry chef, Theodosis Petrou, who had been accused of the murder of Angelos Zemenides in Hampstead in 1933. Petrou fell under suspicion because he had given Zemenides money in his part-time capacity as marriage broker, but Zemenides had found no bride for him and would not return the cash. In Petrou's cellar the police found a .32 calibre Browning automatic hand gun.

Burrard undertook a microscopic comparison of marks on the bullets and cartridges from the crime scene with those he fired himself from the automatic the police had seized. To his surprise, since the police case seemed so powerful, he found that the weapon could not have fired the lethal rounds. And as powerful evidence 'would be required to convince a non-technical jury in view of the damning chain of evidence against the wretched Petrou', he undertook meticulous micro-photography to show how every weapon leaves its own particular 'thumbprint' on the ammunition. The brass cartridge cases, in particular, carry an accurate reverse impression of all the machining marks and any damage or scoring in the breech chamber. The defence claimed that the Browning had been planted in Petrou's premises to incriminate him and he was freed. This was only the second time this type of forensic study had been done in England, though today it is a commonplace notion to enthusiasts for forensic and crime scene investigation dramas on television.[3]

Major Burrard, however, was not the first amateur scientist to study the performance of shotguns in real world conditions for, as he freely conceded, he was following in the footsteps of another great pioneer of this kind of home-grown scientific ballistic science.

In 1913 Sir Ralph Payne-Gallwey published his curiously titled small book *High Pheasants in Theory and Practice*.[4] He had set out, on his estate in Yorkshire, to establish the efficiency of shotguns when fired vertically. As he too noted, gunmakers conducted their trials by firing guns horizontally at whitewashed 'pattern plates' to assess the consistency of the shot pattern of pellets and their penetration. What happened, Payne-Gallwey wondered, in the more usual case, when shooting up in the air? What was the loss of power in the shot charge due to gravity? Would the wind affect the pattern of shot? He made a target frame, 7 feet square and covered with linen, which he had carried aloft by a large kite. 'I had endless trouble,' he recorded, and as might be expected, 'the target whirled around and careered about in a mad fashion, humming as it did so,' while retrieving it as it was lowered was clearly a risky business.[5] However, he did find ways to stabilize the kite-borne target and to record some useful patterns, proving that the power of the gun was considerably reduced by firing upwards against gravity. He was also among the first to quantify the necessity for lead, or forward allowance, calculating that a game bird flew between 2 and 3 m (7–9 ft) during the time of flight of the shot.

The age and the spirit that gave us these ingenious ballistic experiments may seem now impossibly remote and perhaps all these trials smack of originality bordering on the eccentric. But we might reflect that, in the world of arms, this was a time when, in England at least, there was a far closer integration of professional and private interest in

Sir Ralph Payne-Gallwey
at Thirkleby Hall,
Yorkshire (above), and
in his gun room (below).
He was also a passionate
student of the history
of crossbows and early
weapons. The device
under the table may
be a crossbow carriage
or a small model of
a medieval ballista
or siege engine.

arms. Payne-Gallwey died in 1916. In 1914 he had lost his son in one
of the first battles of the Great War. In 1915 the Zeppelin air raids over
England began. Indeed, during 1915 Zeppelins bombed the nearby port
of Hull and he may even have heard them as they roamed freely over
Yorkshire, while the anti-aircraft guns tried to seek them out. Surely
he must have pondered on the dreadful change of events and on how

the sporting problems that had intrigued him had now been translated both to the battlefield and to the preservation of England.

HILL'S BRIGANDS AND THE SCIENCE OF AIR DEFENCE

It seems strange to realize that the first people to fire up into the air were hunters, but of course, until the balloon age and the invention of the aeroplane, there were no airborne military targets. People had shot at observation balloons in the American Civil War and during the siege of Paris in 1870, but it was the invention of the aeroplane that transformed the problem.

The wide diffusion of gun lore had a direct influence too on the conscript citizen armies that Britain fielded in both the First and Second World Wars, and also some transference of technique to the new challenge of shooting down aircraft. It was said, anecdotally, that gamekeepers and shooting men were preferred in the early days for anti-aircraft duty because they intuitively understood the concept of an aiming 'lead'.

Like the pheasant, an aircraft was a tricky target and there were, at the dawn of the craft, no rules and no tables to help the gunner. The first aircraft to be destroyed by gunfire, apparently, was a two-seater of the Austro-Hungarian air force, struck while dropping bombs over the town of Kragujevac in central Serbia, the home to a cannon works and some military installations. The date was 30 September 1915, showing how difficult aircraft were to hit, for this was fully a year after the outbreak of the Great War, since when German, British, Austrian, Italian and Russian aircraft had been droning back and forth unharmed over their respective enemy's lines, spotting and reporting on troop movements and gun emplacements, while the soldiers below filled the sky around them, and probably behind them, with futile clouds of bullets.[6] That day in Kragujevac, however, the Serbian army gunner Radoje Ljutovac somehow estimated the right lead, or forward allowance, by eye, and chose the right moment to fire his Polish-made cannon. Very likely, as a Serbian country boy, he had grown up learning to shoot and hunt. He simply said, 'I believed in my own hand and my artillery experience.'

Reconnaissance from the air was a real threat in the battles in France. The enemy could see weak spots in the line, could shell ammunition dumps and disable gun emplacements, and could see the build-ups of troops and supplies that heralded an attack. The primary task of the famous flying 'aces' with their agile fighter aircraft was not to engage in dogfights with their opposite numbers, although that was the romantic part that captured public attention. Rather, it was to harry, shoot down and deter the slower and relatively helpless two-seat spotter aircraft.

This new kind of reconnaissance was a huge advantage to whichever side had control of the air. But although the 'Archie' (First World War slang for anti-aircraft fire) banged away, most flyers, like Sopwith Camel pilot Victor Yeates, regarded their efforts with relatively detached amusement:

A loud double cough made his heart jump. It was Archie, taking notice of them, and his first shots were always startling if you weren't thinking about him. The black bursts were right in front, and he flew through them and then turned outwards . . . His sudden

Serbian artillery, 1914.

spectral appearances were more surprising than dangerous but it was not advisable to go on flying straight for long when he was active.[7]

It was the arrival of the Zeppelin 'baby killers' over London that really galvanized the anti-aircraft effort. On the night of 31 May 1915 Zeppelins dropped between ninety and one hundred bombs on the east and northeast districts of London. Five people were killed and fourteen injured. Then on 8 September a Zeppelin wandered freely over central London and dropped bombs in Holborn, Farringdon Road and in the City. The attack destroyed numerous buildings and killed 22 civilians, including six children.

Three days after the first Zeppelin attack, the pugnacious naval gunnery expert Admiral Sir Percy Scott (see Chapter Three), now in retirement, was summoned to take over the air defence of London. By some anomaly this was administered by the Admiralty, since the army had apparently washed its hands of it, having committed all its resources to the battle in France. This arrangement was also facilitated by Winston Churchill during his term as First Lord of the Admiralty (the Minister for the navy), who had taken flying lessons and was keenly aware of the new threat posed by aircraft.

To one army officer, just returned from France, the damage to London

> appeared to me . . . to be absolutely negligible. [But] To the inhab-
> itants of London, who had a less intimate acquaintance with the
> effects of high explosives, and who had been brought up to consider
> their island as unapproachable . . . the matter presented itself in
> an entirely different light . . . There was no sign of panic, but . . .
> a deep and universal anger that such attacks could be made upon
> our defenceless women and children.[8]

Scott found a woeful situation: twelve guns defending London and shells with erratic time fuses that did not work. Furthermore, the explosive charge inside the shell was inadequate, the design of the casing was wrong: they did not burst convincingly into fine shrapnel and so the debris would rain down on the capital in large, lethal chunks. For Scott, the government officials he encountered showed all the traits he had spent his naval career fulminating against: 'the maximum amount of apathy and red tapism'. Deciding to emulate the excellent 75 mm guns that the French had mounted on lorries to provide a mobile anti-aircraft defence, Scott asked the Admiralty to get one for him to have copied in Britain: 'This they agreed to see about . . . and I have no doubt that in a few months they would have got the necessary papers through.'[9]

But by good fortune Percy Scott had acquired a highly energetic deputy, Commander Alfred Rawlinson, who had returned home badly injured from war service in France 'after making a somewhat too close acquaintance with a "Jack Johnson" (a large high-calibre high-explosive German shell) during the attack on the Aubers Ridge'.[10] Now fit for home duties, he was chomping at the bit for action and

One of Rawlinson's rapidly made mobile anti-aircraft guns, from Admiral Sir Percy Scott, *Fifty Years in the Royal Navy* (1919). Commander Rawlinson at far left.

Scott, characteristically, skipped ahead of the civil servants by sending Rawlinson, who had been a pre-war racing driver and pioneer aviator, to France to beg, borrow or steal a gun. He left for the ferry, 'going at about fifty miles an hour down South Audley Street', returning in four days to display the gun 'on the Horse Guards Parade, under Mr. Balfour's window, before the official letter asking for it was written'.[11]

Soon Rawlinson's motorized units, with guns and searchlights, were careering around London and through the countryside aiming to get across the track of a Zeppelin when observers spotted one coming over the coast. Their first success was in bringing down Zeppelin L15 off Margate on 1 April 1916. The effects of gunfire and the visible presence of bursting shells soon forced the Zeppelin crews to higher altitudes and to wandering paths around the countryside.

Germany had imagined that the Zeppelin was a new kind of super-technology, the product of a special national scientific talent that less technocratic nations could not emulate. The airships might even over-come sea power and the massive battleships that Britain possessed in ample number might become obsolete in the face of a new kind of fleet. Although slow, they seemed relatively invulnerable when high and could even outclimb fighter aircraft by dropping water ballast. But as the technique of anti-aircraft gunnery improved, and as defending fighters

Zeppelin L33, brought down by gunfire on the night of 23/24 September 1916 at Wigborough, Essex.

Donald Maxwell,
*St George and the
Dragon: Zeppelin L15
in the Thames,
April 1916,* 1917,
oil on canvas.

began to master the dangerous art of night flying, Zeppelin operations became a liability over England and their attacks tailed off.

Perhaps it was fortunate for British defences that Zeppelins, with their huge size and modest speed of about 70 mph, made the first forays over England, for the raids gave a warning that helped establish the equipment and improve the technique. Soon the new Gotha bombing aeroplanes began to come instead. In truth, they were not much faster than Zeppelins at their best, but they were far more manoeuvrable, presented a much smaller target, and were not filled with huge quantities of inflammable hydrogen.

Meanwhile air defence had been becoming far more scientific. In January 1916 the physiologist A. V. Hill received a request from Horace Darwin to collaborate on anti-aircraft research and particularly on the tricky problem of finding the height of an approaching aircraft. Horace was the fifth son of Charles Darwin and founder of the Cambridge Scientific Instrument Company. The two were already acquainted through Hill's scientific work on muscle contraction, and Darwin was aware of Hill's 'unpleasant habit of inventing things'.[12]

Hill was intrigued by the anti-aircraft gunnery problem and, being politically highly adept, managed to detach himself from the Cambridgeshire regiment in which he was musketry officer and began to assemble a group of fellow scientists. What soon became apparent was that no

Sir Charles Holmes, *Awaiting Zeppelins, Sandringham, January 1915*, 1919, oil on canvas. Holmes, subsequently the director of the National Gallery, had been a member of this anti-aircraft crew. Airship activity over Norfolk raised the suspicion that Germany sought to bomb the royal family.

one knew anything about 'high angle' fire and the real path that a projectile took when fired up in the air. As we have seen, seventeenth-century thinkers had developed one theory for ballistic motion that was eventually replaced by the new description embodied in Newtonian mechanics. Since then, practical mathematicians had produced really serviceable sets of rules for gunners firing at land targets. These were combined with 'firing tables' compiled for every type of gun at different elevations and with all the different types of ammunition it might be required to fire. The procedure was that

> when a gun is developed it is taken off to some quiet corner of a proving ground and fired, day after day . . . until a vast amount of data has been amassed as to the range achieved, with various combinations of elevation, shell and cartridge. From this data a firing table is constructed.[13]

Every type of gun has its firing table and this information was collated to enable gunners to hit accurately at (often distant) targets on land (or sea), sometimes even without initial, tell-tale shots to register or calibrate the guns. Since the location of the shell burst could be measured, it gave an unambiguous check on the theory and on the tables. But firing up in the air was a mystery. No one knew where the shell burst, or the path it took to get there.

Hill was a capable mathematician before turning to physiology, but much more mathematical horsepower was needed. First he approached G. H. Hardy, his Cambridge colleague, one of Britain's most eminent mathematicians. Hill recorded that Hardy 'was always an odd fish . . . saying that although he was ready . . . to have his body shot at he was not prepared to prostitute his brains for the purposes of war'. Hardy did, however, propose one of his outstanding students, the future astrophysicist E. A. Milne. 'Apparently,' Hill commented drily, 'he was ready to have Milne's brains prostituted.'[14]

Milne was keen to join. So too was another outstanding Cambridge scholar, the physicist R. H. Fowler, who had returned with a severe wound from the Gallipoli campaign, enabling Hill to snap him up.

Archibald Vivian Hill seated at his desk, 1925. He won the Nobel Prize in Physiology or Medicine in 1922 for work on the mechanism of muscle contraction.

Incidentally, Hardy's partner in theoretical mathematics, J. E. Littlewood, was not so fastidious as Hardy and was quite prepared to analyse artillery problems, locating himself at Woolwich Arsenal, from where he was in touch with Hill about the hitherto unknown science of high-angle trajectories.

In his own discussion of the aesthetics of mathematics, *A Mathematician's Apology*, Hardy expanded a little on this theme: the comforting conclusion that *real* (as opposed to trivial) mathematics has no effect on war. For example, he mused,

> no one has yet found any warlike purpose in the theory of numbers . . . It is true that there are branches of applied mathematics, such as ballistics and aerodynamics which have been developed quite deliberately for war . . . but none of them has any claim to rank as 'real'. They are indeed repulsively ugly and intolerably dull; even Littlewood could not make ballistics respectable, and if he could not, who can? Real mathematics is 'a harmless and innocent occupation . . . So a real mathematician has his conscience clear.'[15]

Hill's group began a wandering existence, first at Northolt aerodrome where the height finder showed its potential, although there was little support from the officers at the aerodrome. Perhaps relics of the pheasant-shooting mentality remained, for Hill recollected that they 'regarded us as cranks, wanting to make a science of a thing intended by nature to remain a sport'.[16] The group moved on to the National Physical Laboratory in Teddington before finally finding an understanding home at the naval gunnery school at the naval station HMS *Excellent* on Whale Island, near Portsmouth.

The first fruit of the group's research was the Hill-Darwin mirror height finder. This used two large mirrors, ruled with squared grids, each with an observer almost a mile apart and communicating by telephone. When each observer simultaneously gave the exact mirror square the aircraft was seen in by each, the height could be calculated by triangulation.

The telephone wire between them had been filched from some other unit, as indeed were most of the experimental team and the scientific people that Hill recruited through personal contacts and unorthodox routes. This unusual crew, in motley uniforms of different services, and some in no military garb at all, rather upset the military establishment. One of the non-uniformed members, William Hartree, was arrested by a military guard while up a telephone pole mending their line and held incommunicado at rifle point for several hours on the assumption that he was trying to communicate with the enemy. There were also attempts to conscript members for army service, particularly E. A. Milne, despite his woefully poor sight. Fortunately, Whale Island was naval property and the commandant, Captain Bowring, was entirely sympathetic and allegedly stationed guards on the bridge to the island to arrest any recruiting sergeants who might try to carry away any of Hill's prize scientific team. Small wonder that the group began to relish their nickname 'Hill's brigands' and soon were granted elaborate

The 'License to practise as a Brigand' was modelled on a hybrid of an OBE and a Home Office vivisection certificate.

job titles – principal this and principal that, according to rank (Milne was an 'Unprincipled Brigand') – the whole laid out in a cod-heraldic 'License to practise as a Brigand' in antique script and modelled on a hybrid of an OBE and a Home Office vivisection certificate. It was accompanied by a cartoon of medieval ground-to-air fire: a crossbow shooting at an incoming dragon.

The Hill-Darwin height finder proved remarkably accurate in measuring the height of aircraft, but perhaps its greatest contribution was in helping to confirm the true flight characteristics of anti-aircraft shells. Since no one really knew the height at which the shrapnel shells exploded, the mirror height finder was used to establish this by spotting the smoke puffs that occurred when they burst. Successive firings with different fuse settings could also establish the paths that the shells took on their way.

Meanwhile E. A. Milne worked on formulae to establish the effects of decreasing barometric pressure as the shell climbed and also investigated the change in temperature with altitude, in case this was one cause of the erratic burning of their time fuse. As a bookish, short-sighted scholar he showed great enterprise by going aloft in two-seaters and taking temperature and pressure measurements up to 4,420 m (14,500 ft) and, incidentally, being one of the early observers to record the effects of lack of oxygen. 'We bottomed 10°F of frost. Heavens but it was cold, but heavens, how I enjoyed it! . . . My pilots both became jocular when at the top – one started singing.'[17]

The Brigands were also curious about the variability of the wind layers as the shell climbed (all new knowledge) and its actual strength at high altitude. They had a graphic illustration of it one day when a large piece of steel shrapnel from a shell, fired by the group to 6,100 m (20,000 ft) off Whale Island, travelled a full mile to land on Hayling Island golf links, 'much to the astonishment of an old gentleman and his wife who were standing nearby'. The near-victim found his way to the gunners with the jagged relic. They thanked him profusely for his kindness in bringing it back, saying that it was 'a piece of shrapnel case that they had lost and he had made a very valuable observation . . . But

Cartoon received by all the Brigands. While 'Ye Squyre of ye Ordnance' waits to give the command to fire the crossbow, wizards consult 'Ye Gadgett' – the height finder – and 'Ye Treatise'.

this did not really appear to satisfy him.'[18] The gentleman's indignation was quite reasonable, for some 135 people are estimated to have been killed during the war in Britain by falling 'friendly' anti-aircraft shell fragments.

In the end Milne's procedures for averaging out pressure and wind speed at different altitudes, combined with Littlewood's revised ballistics, were verified by observation and the height finder instruments. The work of the group served as the basis for the *Textbook of Anti-aircraft Gunnery* published for the War Office in 1925. This was still the standard work when war came again in 1939, and though there were new factors to absorb, like mass night bombing, higher aircraft speeds and the new technique of radar, the ballistic part of the problem had essentially been solved by the Brigands.

In the post-war period Hill returned to physiology, winning the Nobel Prize in Physiology or Medicine in 1922 for his work on muscle contraction. Milne had been awarded a Fellowship at Trinity College, Cambridge, in 1910 and became a distinguished astrophysicist (among other work he established a method for determining the temperatures of stars). Unusually he won the fellowship to the college despite having never completed his degree, but the war years with the Brigands had amply completed his education in physics and in the technique of scientific research. He recalled that:

> At directing research, both [A. V. Hill and R. H. Fowler] were superb . . . To behold the way they set about a new problem, often in a new terrain with new material, to see the way they made inferences and came to conclusions and sound judgements and to take part in it all, was far better training than most Universities can offer to aspirants in research . . . [My] three years' period under Hill and Fowler, at the most formative period of [my] life . . . was a most vivid, enjoyable and valuable experience; to both of them [I] can never be sufficiently grateful for that schooling.[19]

ANTI-AIRCRAFT FIRE AND THE SECOND WORLD WAR

Perhaps the most intriguing legacy of the Brigands lay in the response of British science to the Second World War. History has tended to personalize this to an extreme degree, tending to depict all scientific advice as flowing through Winston Churchill's confidant and close adviser Frederick Lindemann (Lord Cherwell). In fact, A. V. Hill played a crucial and early role, although he never gained the ear of Churchill and, in fact, campaigned actively against what he considered to be Lindemann's undue influence.

Long before Churchill came back from the wilderness to take control of the Admiralty in September 1939, and to become Prime Minister in the following year, Hill had been at hard work to try to ensure that, unlike during the previous war, scientists should be used in a rational way across the whole military field, and not find their way to military problems by haphazard and roundabout routes, or, even worse, be consumed as cannon fodder again in the trenches.

Now, using his position as Secretary of the Royal Society, Hill became the driving force behind creating a reference list of all scientists according to their specialisms. In 1938 Hill was writing urgently from the Royal Society, chivvying vice-chancellors and administrators at every university to list all their scientific staff and students, past and present. 'Hitler does not give one much time,' he urged. When war broke out, a year later, there were 7,000 names on the list, now known as the 'Central Register', a 'precision instrument' that was used to make the best use of the scientists throughout the war and helped to match skill and knowledge with all the emerging military and social problems of an unprecedentedly technical war.[20]

But in spite of the authoritarian and Orwellian ring of its title, the Central Register was not Hill's only tool since, thanks in part to the Brigands, Hill was well connected at high levels with the military and with government. At any rate, personal connections and 'string-pulling' still remained an essential feature of integrating science with war. Hill saw that anti-aircraft defence was one of the most pressing problems of

The Vickers predictor –
a complex single-purpose
electromechanical
analogue computer for
anti-aircraft guns, 1940.

Detail of the Vickers
predictor. This predictor
is one of a considerable
number manufactured
in the USA by the Sperry
Gyroscope Company.

the war and, as attacks started, sought out General 'Tim' Pile, head of the anti-aircraft command, who agreed that the problem needed both scientific analysis and 'the quick intuition of a freshman'.[21]

Anti-aircraft fire, as Pile was the first to admit, was not doing very well. The problems, of course, were very similar to the ones that Hill had tangled with in the First World War, except that the speed of enemy aircraft had doubled, their flying height had increased – and there were many more of them. Furthermore, as the air battles of 1940 progressed, the bomber formations began to come by night. In the First World War it could be necessary to aim almost a kilometre ahead of an enemy 'scout' to arrange for the shell and the aeroplane to arrive in the same piece of space in the same instant. By the Second World War, with vastly increased speeds and heights, the aiming lead might need to be some 6.5 km (4 mi.) ahead. This could seem so counter-intuitive to the gun crew on heavy AA guns that the gun layers and the fuse setter sometimes sat with their backs to the target in order to prevent their glancing up at the aircraft, simply matching the pointers on their dials for elevation, bearing and fuse height to the settings directed by the predictor mechanism.

There was now, however, a new, helpful development since the First World War – the anti-aircraft predictor. This was an electro-mechanical analogue computer that integrated the aircraft speed, its height and its 'track' or compass heading to compute a 'firing solution', determining the gun elevation, its bearing and the fuse setting (for the height of the burst). These were read off from three separate dials and, at first, the guns were set manually by their crews from this data.

A second helpful invention was radar. But although the giant radar towers that ringed the coast (Chain Home) were excellent for detecting raids and for helping the war rooms direct fighters to the raiders, they were not precise enough for the pinpoint location that the guns needed. Fortunately the same boffins had been at work on a finer instrument working on a shorter wavelength and christened GL (for gun-laying) radar. The crash programme had produced serviceable sets but, when the war came, they had not yet been properly married to the predictor systems that had been designed to use precise optical bearings.

In 1940 A. V. Hill took Pile to a meeting of the Royal Society, where the physicist Patrick Blackett was speaking. Pile was very impressed with him and remarked, 'why should I not have that chap Blackett?'[22]

Blackett was an ideal intermediary between science and the military for he was not an ordinary scientist. Although he gained the Nobel Prize for his work on the nuclear disintegration of atoms, before turning to physics he had been a junior officer on board HMS *Barham* at the Battle of Jutland in 1916, and later the gunnery officer on a destroyer. Blackett did not imagine that scientists knew better than military personnel, with all their bitterly won personal experience, but he argued that tactics should

Patrick Blackett had been a young naval officer at the Battle of Jutland in the First World War before becoming a physicist. He won the Nobel Prize in Physics for work on atomic disintegration and cosmic rays. In the Second World War, he became one of the founders of operational research – the application of science to military operations. Photograph by Howard Coster, c. 1935.

be informed by statistical analysis and by longer runs of data than could easily be accumulated by combat personnel in individual engagements. In addition, he held that 'success in most operations of war in general, and almost all operations of air war, is due to the sum of a number of small victories, for each of which the chance of success in a given operation is small.'[23]

'British Weapons to Defeat Hitler', Second World War poster, 1942–5.

A British Anti-aircraft Battery in action. More than 590 German raiders have been destroyed by anti-aircraft fire over Britain.

Blackett saw that the quite understandable wish for new weapons might sometimes be a kind of escapism. He parodied this as: 'our present equipment doesn't work very well . . . Let's have a new gadget.' Of course, the gadget might take a year to arrive, and even then might have its own limitations. So how could the success of all the equipment that was actually available be maximized? This thought was at the heart of the new science of operational research, which Blackett did so much to originate.

Many of Blackett's most brilliant successes involved the subtle optimization of a range of factors in the whole weapons system, along the whole complex chain of events running from detection to attack. Blackett and his scientific recruits, who quickly became known as 'Blackett's circus', quickly improved the performance of AA fire. They

'A British Anti-aircraft Battery in Action', Second World War poster, 1942–5.

helped show how the newly available early warning tracks from radar, though still relatively imprecise, could be smoothed and married to the existing fire-control predictors on the guns, and calculated the best placings and groupings for the guns on the basis of statistics and probabilities.

In the early stages of the war, much of the night-time AA gunfire was fired using a very imprecise location of the target, and though Churchill liked people to hear the sound of the guns during raids, he was worried

The 94-mm (3.7 in.) gun of the 127th Heavy Anti-Aircraft Regiment, Southwold, Suffolk, 9 October 1944.

Visiting an AA site: General Pile, Winston Churchill and Churchill's daughter Mary, who was a corporal in one of General Pile's anti-aircraft batteries.

about the prodigious use of ammunition. Perhaps a greater worry was that AA Command was wearing out the barrels of its guns faster than the stretched industrial suppliers could replace them.

The 'rounds per bird' (the AA gunners still used that expression), however, quickly fell from 20,000 shells fired per aircraft destroyed to 4,000 according to one estimate. Moreover, during the Battle of Britain anti-aircraft fire destroyed some three hundred German aircraft (General Pile estimated 357) out of the 1,630 shot down, an important contribution to victory.

The anti-aircraft command became a highly progressive service. Among its many challenges, moving the guns to counter expected raids was a major effort. General Pile was perhaps the only commander to keep his senior post throughout the war and early on, despite some opposition, introduced women into front-line service, also arguing that women doing the same work should receive the same pay.

U.S. Air Force B-24 over Germany in the Second World War, emerging from a cloud of anti-aircraft fire. The smoke puffs show that by 1945 the estimation of height for the AA gunnery was almost perfect in Germany as well as with the Allies. But although the aircraft has been struck in one starboard engine, there are still 'holes in the pattern' that it has flown through.

By 1945 anti-aircraft fire had become remarkably accurate (and the reasons will become apparent in the next chapter). But whether it was due to the still challenging task of hitting aircraft, or the conceptual antecedents of anti-aircraft gunnery in the art of shooting game birds on the wing, anti-aircraft personnel still retained a remarkably spry attitude to their craft. Heavy anti-aircraft crews were not generally subject to the fearful experiences of the field gunners or tank men who risked annihilation, duelling directly against each other in a game of lethal speed. The sporting spirit of anti-aircraft personnel in the Second World War is conveyed in rare memoirs such as *How We Lived and Laughed (with the 195)*. Even though the 195th Heavy Anti-Aircraft Battery took its weapons to hellish battle cauldrons like Mersa Matruh, El Alamein and Tobruk, the author's impish relish was clearly undimmed:

> Now I'll tell you a tale of the battle,
> The battle of Mersah Matruh
> Of the glorious stand of the 195
> And a glorious bolt from the blue
>
> Two thousand rounds we disposed of,
> Two thousand rounds without boast,
> The barrels were red hot in places
> And Leonard got cracking on toast.[24]

Of course, this relative immunity of heavy AA batteries did not apply to shipborne gunners or to those manning lighter, close-range weapons used for the local defence of army sites and airfields. Here, of course, the gunner was as much a target as the assets he was protecting, and the need for reactive, fast and accurate anti-aircraft fire would prove to be a spur to developments in electronics, computers and communications theory of a profound and transformatory kind.

5

FIRE CONTROL AND
A NEW SCIENCE OF LIFE

Shortly after the Second World War a Polish gunner fighting with the Allied forces set down an intriguing impression of his anti-aircraft battery. He recalled that when the gun barrels began to traverse onto a target guided by its predictor mechanism, 'they looked like four huge serpents getting ready to strike'.[1]

Had he known of it, this observation would certainly have tickled the interest of Norbert Wiener, the American mathematician, polymath and inventor of the new science that he christened 'cybernetics'. Wiener's research during the Second World War had been devoted to anti-aircraft gunnery and what Americans called the 'fire control problem'. This brought him into contact with a high-powered group of control engineers and theoreticians devoted to making anti-aircraft guns, with their servo mechanisms and radar, more responsive, more autonomous and, as it would turn out, more 'lifelike'.

To our gunner, the choreography of the guns, swinging onto line and rearing up like a cobra, recalled a living creature precisely because the system had indeed been given some (albeit a very simple set) of the reactive properties of living things. And from this ensemble – the radar, predictor, the servos and the gun battery – there arose the new science of cybernetics, bringing with it a profound and irreversible effect on the way we perceive our humanity.

THE ANTI-AIRCRAFT PROBLEM

The Second World War brought new and intense analysis to the dynamic control of guns. The inefficiency of the anti-aircraft gun was, we have seen, underlined by the immense expenditure of ammunition during the Battle of Britain in 1940 (see Chapter Four). Later, at Pearl Harbor in 1941, the Japanese Navy launched 354 aircraft from their carriers during the attack for the loss of only 29 in spite of heavy anti-aircraft fire.[2] These events were a powerful spur to research in the USA and the UK.

Control engineering for production and manufacturing had been a growing subject in American industry during the 1930s. Control engineers, academics and electronics experts now converged on a programme divided between the recently formed Radiation Laboratory (the famous RadLab) at the Massachusetts Institute of Technology (MIT) and the research centre of the Bell Telephone Company.[3] The challenge was to solve the pressing problem of getting anti-aircraft guns to track fast targets dynamically and accurately, using the newly invented technique of radar.[4] The RadLab devised the radar component, while the analogue computer came from Bell.

An anti-aircraft battery in the early and middle stages of the war combined three elements: the battery (a group of guns usually slaved together and moving as one), a dedicated radar set, and the computer that took inputs for speed, height and range of the target in order to calculate the aiming point ahead of the aircraft. This computer was called, in the UK, the predictor, though Americans called it, with perhaps more confidence, the director.

Initially these three elements were served and linked by a human crew. The challenge was to improve the system and to eliminate this chain of human 'repeaters' and gun-layers so that the radar output would go directly to the computer and from it to servo-motors that automatically trained the guns in response to its calculations. The result was a remarkable automatic weapons system, the SCR 584 (for Signal Corps Radio), which by 1944 could destroy about 70 per cent of the VI flying bombs passing over the guns in southern England and also proved

View of Pearl Harbor during the raid, with anti-aircraft shell bursts overhead, 7 December 1941. The large column of smoke in lower centre is from USS *Arizona*. In spite of this lethal-looking barrage of anti-aircraft shell bursts, this fire, aimed by human gun-layers, was strikingly ineffective. Only 29 Japanese aircraft were hit out of 354 attackers.

Photograph of sailors on a motor launch rescuing a survivor from the burning USS *West Virginia* (BB-48) in Pearl Harbor, 7 December 1941. At least seven torpedoes struck the ship, and two bombs pierced the outer hull but failed to detonate.

invaluable to the U.S. Navy for battleship and aircraft carrier defence in the Pacific War. These anti-aircraft gunnery sets were probably the ultimate achievement of the emerging field of artificial intelligence during the Second World War, since most other advanced technologies, for example sonar (or ASDIC in British usage) and the long-range early warning radar sets used for national defence, were still critically dependent on skilled human interpreters to filter the results and to separate significant signals from spurious ones and 'noise' at that stage in their development.

The whole anti-aircraft gunnery system had now become an integrated electronic and mechanical ensemble, but the essential insight was the realization that control could be made far more exact if the guns signalled their actual position back to the computer, as well as the rate at which they were approaching the required position. The engineering term for this kind of information is 'feedback'.

Feedback was the key to performance. Most control systems in the pre-war world were 'command' systems or, as the control theorists would come to term it, 'open loop'. The principle is that the operator makes a control input, for example turning the wheel that moves the cutting tool of a lathe, and so the cutting tool moves to a certain position. The accuracy of this relies on the initial calibration of the system and on the accuracy of every joint or linkage, and this inevitably degrades over time. All mechanical devices have some looseness in their linkages, usually called 'slop' or 'backlash': and so much better performance results

Drawing of SCR-584 with gun battery: mobile medium-range microwave anti-aircraft artillery gun-laying set (AA), consisting of semi-trailer and 4-ton tractor.

An experimental truck (xt-1) housing the scr-584.

if a machine tool or a gun has local measuring devices to signal back to the computer exactly where it is at any moment. This is feedback and it means that the gun can decelerate subtly as it approaches the desired bearing and stop exactly without error, overshooting or 'hunting', in spite of the mass and inertia of the guns. This is very much what humans do when we reach for a glass, or an egg. Position sensors (propriocep-tors in the muscles and tendons) slow and stop the arm and hand with infinite subtlety so we can move fast but can seize a fragile object with incredible precision.

Norbert Wiener worked on mathematical aspects of the gunnery problem and particularly on the statistical prediction of the likely evasive movements of aircraft targets. However, his top-secret mathematical report seemed needlessly abstruse and indigestible to the more pragmatic control engineers. One anecdotal remark was the harsh suggestion that 'the best use for it would be to give it to the enemy while [we] get on with winning the war.'

Norbert Wiener at MIT
in the 1950s.

Nevertheless, he did something that had not occurred to these engineers, for he sensed that radar-directed gunnery system pointed to a way of studying humans and all living creatures that used sensing and feedback for control. The result was his formulation of the subject of cybernetics, a study of the web of sensing, control, communication and movement in purposeful machines – a subject that he considered to be really a new science of life, which could be deployed on social, economic and even psychiatric problems.[5]

For him, the anti-aircraft gun set could be thought of as modelling a biological organism with a sensory system (the radar), a brain (the computer or predictor) and a gun, to be directed like the arm and hand. Or, put another way, mechanisms had started to converge with living systems and it seemed they could begin to provide rich insights into biology, movement and control. As part of this study Wiener began to collaborate with the Mexican neurophysiologist Arturo Rosenblueth to understand more about nervous control and feedback in human beings, and they continued this association in their post-war work.

As the detailed design of the new anti-aircraft gun systems progressed, new problems of integrating the radar sets, computers, servo-motors and all the mechanical elements emerged and the biological parallel seemed increasingly apt. For example, the ensemble could choke on information, 'hunting' or oscillating in a useless way if not matched properly.

This was extremely intriguing to Wiener and Rosenblueth because it seemed that the afflictions of these newly invented machines mirrored known human neurological conditions, for example the 'intention tremors' caused by some kinds of brain damage in which a patient's hand swings more the closer it approaches the desired object. This, Wiener noted, was 'an oscillation in the goal-seeking process that occurs only when that process is actively invoked . . . for example, when the patient reaches for a glass of water, his hand swings wider and wider, and he cannot lift up the glass.' Wiener also observed that

> there is another type of human tremor which is in some ways diametrically opposite to intention tremor. It is known as Parkinsonianism, and is familiar to all of us as the shaking palsy of old men. Here the patient displays the tremor even at rest, and, in fact, if the disease is not too greatly marked, only at rest. When he attempts to accomplish a definite purpose this tremor subsides, to such an extent that the victim of an early stage of Parkinsonianism can even be a successful eye surgeon.[6]

These human conditions seemed to mirror some of the 'diseases of the guns' that development engineers had met with during the anti-aircraft development project – malfunctions that resulted, for example, from feedback rates that were too high or inappropriate levels of signal amplification. These parallels between apparently analogous symptoms in humans and mechanisms seemed to confirm cybernetics as a source of real insight. To explore these ideas Wiener and colleagues built artificial animals they christened Moth and Bedbug: light-seeking and light-avoiding machines that were electronically adjustable for feedback and amplification patterns so they could exhibit either type of tremor.

'Moth' was, in fact, studied by the United States Army Medical Corps to compare with human cases of nervous tremor.

Norbert Wiener had early training as a prodigy, being educated at home with methods invented by his domineering father, a professor of Slavic languages and literature at Harvard. Interviewed, aged eleven, for the front page of *The World* magazine under the title 'The Most Remarkable Boy in the World', he went on to become the youngest PhD in Harvard history and then to Trinity College, Cambridge, as a post-doctoral researcher tutored by Bertrand Russell. This did not work out well and Russell, then the great man in British mathematical philosophy, caviled at indulging 'the infant prodigy named Wiener . . . The youth has been flattered, and thinks himself God Almighty – there is a perpetual contest between him and me as to which is to do the teaching.'[7]

For his part, Wiener formed 'a great dislike for Russell', writing home that 'I feel a detestation for the man . . . his mind impresses me as a keen, cold, narrow logical machine, that cuts the universe into neat little packets, that measure, as it were, were, just three inches each way.'[8] In retrospect, though, he described Russell more indulgently, crediting him with providing a grounding in mathematical logic, and recalling him almost fondly as 'looking then, as he does now, like the Mad Hatter'.

Wiener launched his novel ideas with the paper 'Behavior, Purpose and Teleology', written in collaboration with Rosenblueth and the engineer Julian Bigelow, which, provokingly, they published in a philosophical journal.[9] The central, disruptive proposition was that some machines could (now) be regarded as having intentions and purposeful behaviour. They argued that, essentially, 'intention' was not just an attribute of conscious beings; machines, like guided weapons, that used feedback were also purposeful.[10]

The full exposition came in 1948 with the publication of his book *Cybernetics; or, Control and Communication in the Animal and the Machine*.[11] Two years later he expanded his analysis to discuss the internal signalling systems of these machines, again challenging the idea of human specialness with the assertion that language is not an exclusive attribute of man, but is one which he may share to a certain degree with the machines he has constructed . . . In a certain sense, all communication systems terminate in machines, but the ordinary communications systems of language terminate in the rather special sort of machine known as a human being.[12]

This formulation could have been seen as highly contentious. If 'language' implies communication between thinking entities, the use of 'information language' is surely objectionable on philosophical grounds. Why, for example, with gunnery control, should we accept the word 'message' and not insist on more rigorous terms like 'error signal' or 'position indication'? Nevertheless, Wiener and the other cyberneticians succeeded remarkably easily in introducing notions of language and information into other branches of science and into everyday life. Fortuitously, in 1948 Claude Shannon also introduced his revelatory theory of information. It was now just 'a small step to think about information as a kind of bodiless fluid that could flow between different substrates without loss of meaning or form.'[13]

Partly through this new work, and through personal wartime experience with codes, ciphers and the transmission and processing of signals, the language of information also spread rapidly into biology. The post-war take-off in molecular biology was energized by ideas about information. For example, the emergence of ideas on the structure of DNA and its function in genetic coding was clearly infused with the spirit of information science and cybernetics.[14]

It was only later that some writers, and principally Lily Kay, began to question the routine use of the metaphor of language in what were really mechanistic, chemical and biological events, noting 'the problem of linguistic signification without human agency or semantics' and quoting the objection from geneticist Philippe L'Héritier that 'being a symbolic language, human language presupposes an interlocutor and a comprehending brain but in genetic language we have nothing but information transfer between molecules . . . and even then, "information transfer" is just a metaphor.'[15]

Nevertheless, the language of information is seductively appropriate to molecular biology (and today has even entered the armoury of quantum physics) and perhaps now only a pedant would quarrel with terms like 'instruction', 'language' and even 'intention' with reference to machines.[16] Our sense of the appropriateness of such words is, ultimately, not so much an intellectual or philosophical judgement but one really based on empathy, or perhaps on recognition.

LAUNCHING CYBERNETICS

Wiener's claim was that cybernetics had a universality that could be applied to all complex systems. For a while it was hugely influential, promising a revolution in psychiatry, a new science of mind and consciousness, and a means for understanding social organizations, businesses and the politics of nations. Wiener travelled and wrote extensively, aided by the polymathic psychoneurologist Warren McCulloch.[17]

As a young student at Haverford College, near Philadelphia, McCulloch was asked what he wanted to achieve in his studies. He replied that all he wanted to know was: 'What is a number that a man may know it; and a man, that he may know a number?' His professor, the Quaker philosopher Rufus Jones, replied, 'Friend, thee will be busy as long as thee lives.' Progressing through psychology and neurophysiology, McCulloch worked in clinical areas on tremors and Parkinsonism, considered feedback in amplifiers as a possible model for brain function and also became familiar with emerging information theory. In 1943 McCulloch encountered *The Nature of Explanation* by the Cambridge psychologist and philosopher Kenneth Craik, 'which I read five times before I realized why Einstein said it was a great book'.

He also began to consider the brain in terms of neural networks and, noting that neurons operate in a binary way, either resting or 'firing' a voltage pulse, saw a parallel with logic gates, the switchgear at the heart of the newly emerging world of digital computers. Then, probably in 1941, he met Norbert Wiener and 'was amazed at Norbert's exact knowledge, pointed questions and clear thinking on neurophysiology. He also talked of various kinds of computation and was happy with my notion of brains as, to a first guess, digital computers.'[18]

McCulloch was excited by the new cybernetic ideas, proclaiming that 'our adventure is actually a great heresy. We are about to conceive of the knower as a computing machine.'[19] He hubristically noted that

> even James Clerk Maxwell who wanted nothing more than to know the relations between thoughts and the molecular motions of the brain cut short his query with the memorable phrase; 'but does not the way to it lie through the very den of the metaphysician, strewn with the bones of former explorers and abhorred by every man of science'.[20]

Cybernetics, in the minds of its creators, was nothing less ambitious than a new science of life and Wiener and McCulloch provokingly signposted their offices in MIT as 'The Department of Experimental Epistemology'. Philosophy, it implied, was now redundant. The ancient problems of knowledge, sensation, perception and intention would now be solved by experimental machines, electronic valves, model circuits and computers.

Warren McCulloch later in life.

McCulloch proved to be the second prophet of cybernetics, launching the influential Macy Foundation conferences in New York to promote it (they ran from 1944 to 1953). He was also the first president of the American Cybernetic Society and, although Alan Turing reputedly thought him a charlatan, his papers are considered classics in the emerging field of cognitive science. As an aid to thought about mental events he also trialled the idea of the 'psychon', meant to be the analogue of the atom, an irreducible quantum of mental activity – 'the simplest psychic act'. Intriguingly, and in spite of what has been achieved in recent years with brain imaging, nothing so atomistic has been glimpsed.

BRITISH CYBERNETICS AND THE RATIO CLUB

Although cybernetics burst onto the world as an American invention, in the UK biologists and neurophysiologists had collaborated with physicists and engineers on problems of gun-aiming, piloting and on radar and electronic systems, and 'information' had come to acquire a special and more technical meaning.

But unfortunately no one individual had the chutzpah (the word is particularly appropriate to Wiener) to name and to sell the wartime insights as a new science. Perhaps the nearest equivalent to Wiener in the UK would have been the brilliant Scottish psychologist Kenneth Craik. Craik was an early thinker about cognitive psychology and a philosopher who became involved in the study of human/machine interfaces because of the war. His work, as we have seen, had previously impressed McCulloch, but tragically he was killed in a cycling accident in Cambridge on the last day of the war.[21]

Partly piqued by the success of Wiener's book, John Bates, a London-based neurologist who had done war research with Craik, started canvassing interest for a dining-club to discuss cybernetics in 1949. This became known as the Ratio Club, based mainly at the National Hospital for Nervous Diseases at Queen Square in Bloomsbury. Bates wrote to one prospective member that

> you might be interested in a dining-club that I am forming to talk 'Cybernetics' occasionally with beer and full bellies. My idea was to have a strictly limited membership . . . half primarily phys-iologists and psychologists, though with electrical leanings, and half primarily communication theory and electrical folk though with biological leanings and all who I know have been thinking 'Cybernetics' before Wiener's book appeared.[22]

He reflected that 'those who have been influenced by these ideas so far, would not acknowledge any particular indebtedness to Wiener, for although he was the first to collect them under one cover, they had been common knowledge to many workers in biology who had contacts with various types of engineering during the war.'[23]

There was, no doubt, an element of anti-Americanism here – or perhaps envy of the American researcher's celebrity and generous research funding. The highlight of an early meeting was to be the attendance of Wiener's associate Warren McCulloch. Bates, however, wrote to Grey Walter, the electro-physiologist and a key member, that

I had led myself to expect too much of McCulloch and was a little disappointed; partly for the reason that I find all Americans less clever than they appear to think themselves; partly because I discovered by hearing him talk on 6 occasions . . . that he had chunks of his purple stuff stored up parrot-wise.[24]

Left to right:
W. Ross Ashby, Warren McCulloch, Grey Walter and Norbert Wiener, at the cybernetics conference in Paris, January 1951. In his book *Thinking by Machine* (*La Pensée artificielle*, 1953), Pierre de Latil captioned the picture 'The four pioneers of cybernetics'.

Even a visit from the master himself had failed to impress Grey Walter, who wrote that

> We had a visit yesterday from Professor Wiener . . . I . . . find his views somewhat difficult to absorb, but he represents quite a large group in the States, including McCulloch and Rosenblueth. These people are thinking on very much the same lines as Kenneth Craik did, but with much less sparkle and humour.[25]

The Ratio Club provided a powerful spur to post-war research in Britain and extended its influence across many disciplines. Alan Turing was a member, as was John Pringle, who had been active in airborne radar research in the UK. For Pringle, 'the club was unique . . . it was invaluable in getting me back into biological research after the war.'[26] Pringle, who was returning to zoology, succeeded in recording electrical signals from the tiny nerves of insects – the first time this had been done – a virtuoso experiment that again highlighted the close connection between wartime defence electronics and fundamental research in the post-war era.

ARTIFICIAL LIFE: TORTOISES AND BRAINS

One day in August 1951, Alan Turing set out for the Festival of Britain with Cambridge colleagues, including his friend Robin Gandy. First they visited the Science Museum in South Kensington, which housed the festival's display of science and technology. They were amused by the cybernetic 'tortoises' developed by the neurologist and Ratio Club member Grey Walter. There were two, Elsie and Elmer, and each of these bumbling 'proto-robots' was fitted with light and a photo-receptor, so they appeared to dance together clumsily when they caught sight of each other across their enclosure. The tortoises were particularly unresponsive that day and Gandy joked that the one named Elmer appeared to be suffering from general paralysis of the insane (the condition associated with the terminal stage of syphilis).

The circuitry of the machines was impertinently simple, reflecting their inventor's view that wartime advances in electronics had brought intelligent, reactive, 'cybernetic' machinery closer and that human intelligence would soon be understood. Indeed, when the tortoises were on form they seemed capable of generating quite provoking and surprisingly lifelike behaviour, leading Grey Walter to express the conviction that the complexity of the brain 'was not so great'.[27]

Grey Walter held a special place in propagandizing for artificial intelligence and in the development of cybernetics in Britain. In contrast to the 'cultured objectivity' of British science, he was a colourful figure who 'cultivated a more swashbuckling image as an emotional adventurer [with] a heterogenous series of roles ranging from robotics pioneer, home guard explosives expert, wife-swapper, TV-pundit, experimental drugs user . . . to anarcho-syndicalist champion of leucotomy and electro-convulsive therapy'.[28]

Beyond cybernetics, his main professional contribution was to electro-encephalography, for he was an expert experimenter and electronic equipment designer devising techniques for recording and classifying the electrical activity of the brain such as alpha and theta

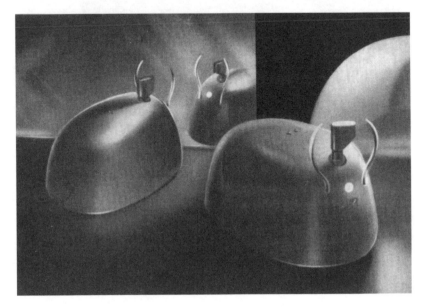

Grey Walter's tortoises: 'Mechanical "animals" can be made to steer themselves towards the light,' from the 1951 Festival of Britain exhibition catalogue.

waves. He was also adept at modifying and adapting electronic apparatus. In the post-war era, much equipment that had previously been rare and expensive, such as cathode ray oscilloscopes for displaying waves, voltages and transient electrical events, now became cheaply available as government war surplus and Grey Walter adapted it, observing that 'the equipment used today for studying brain activity contains many parts and devices which were developed for radar apparatus during the war.'[29]

But the dominion of wartime electronics went far beyond technique and seemed to suggest mechanistic explanations for the baffling electrical phenomena of the brain. Inspired directly by this radar experience, Grey Walter suggested that the alpha wave was a kind of scanning

RAF display unit for the 'Gee' bomber navigation unit from Grey Walter's laboratory, 1946–9. This was the type of war-surplus equipment he modified to show fine-scale electrical events in the brain.

Internal arrangement of the tortoise, without carapace, at the Burden Neurological Institute, c. 1950.

process in the brain, a thought that he explored further with the vision system for his tortoises.

These devices were really rhetorical toys, small battery-powered three-wheel devices with two sensors. In the context of cybernetics, however, they were electronic arguments for Grey Walter's take on lifelike intelligence and behaviour. The scanning he referred to was achieved by mounting a sensor (a photo-electric cell) on top of a rotating vertical shaft, which also carried the single front steering wheel on the bottom end. The rear wheels drove the device forwards or in reverse while the photocell and the wheel rotated together, continually causing the machine to roll along with a kind of looping motion until it 'sighted' a light source, which immediately suppressed the rotation of the cell, giving the machine a destination. However, contact with an obstacle closed a switch under the shell and caused the tortoise to reverse direction. And so its behaviour was produced by a continual and varying combination of these built-in properties: attraction to light, and repulsion by contact.

Each tortoise could follow a light, reverse from physical obstacles, and Elsie could even reverse into a 'hutch' for charging when batteries ran low. As each was fitted with a headlight, they could also attract each other. However, they could never consummate their 'desire' since physical contact gave a check, and each backed away, only to repeat the cycle of attraction and repulsion, producing a curious dance that might continue indefinitely unless an external light source proved more attractive, when both would break off to pursue it.

Grey Walter interpreted this futile mating dance as evidence of mutual recognition. However, one tortoise by itself also generated intriguing behaviour when faced with a mirror, since the reflection of the machine's own light attracted it via the photocell. Of course, bumping into the mirror caused it to reverse away, only to undergo the same cycle of attraction and retreat, repeatedly 'flickering, twittering and jigging like a clumsy Narcissus'. If this behaviour were to be observed in an animal, Grey Walter reflected, 'it might be accepted as evidence of some degree of self-awareness.'[30]

Like Norbert Wiener, Grey Walter situated his robots in the world of air attack and weaponry, recalling that

> the first notion of constructing a free goal-seeking mechanism goes back to a wartime talk with the psychologist Kenneth Craik . . . Goal-seeking missiles were literally much in the air in those days; so [too] in our minds were scanning mechanisms . . . the two ideas . . . combined as the essential mechanical conception of a working model that would behave like a simple animal.[31]

These tortoises were the source of much of Grey Walter's celebrity and attracted immense press coverage. The heady cybernetic atmosphere in Britain at the time was recorded by the French author Pierre de Latil, who encountered the tortoises in Grey Walter's home near Bristol:

> Elsie moved to and fro just like a real animal . . . I enclosed Elsie in a barricade of furniture, but by banging herself and reversing

and knocking and backing and turning again, she managed to find her way out . . .

'We mustn't keep her waiting for her meal much longer', said Grey Walter . . . On the floor was a sort of hutch illuminated by a very strong lamp inside it. Immediately Elsie made off towards it . . . There was a faint click and Elsie remained motionless . . . leaning against the contacts at the back of the hutch . . . 'She is taking her bottle,' said Grey Walter.[32]

Grey Walter was in the habit of shamelessly anthropomorphizing his tortoises for rhetorical purposes. Although the machines might be

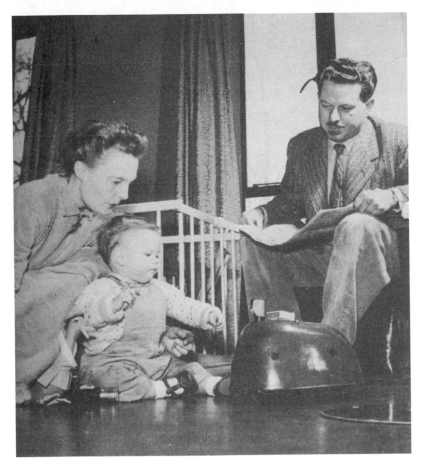

Grey Walter with Vivian Dovey and their son, Timothy. In his book *Thinking by Machine* (1953), Pierre de Latil recorded that 'in their country home near Bristol, these parents have two children: one is electronic . . . Timothy is very friendly with his mechanized sister.'

The magus of the machine: Grey Walter in his sitting room with Elmer and Elsie, April 1950. He wrote to Norbert Wiener that 'we have included features . . . which give [the tortoises] . . . an exploratory and ethical attitude to the universe as well as a purely tropistic one.' Placing a lit candle on each one and using a long exposure allowed Larry Burrows of *Life* magazine to capture the looping paths of the devices.

made up merely of switches, batteries, motors and wires, so too, this language implied, were we. And Elsie could have appetites too, as, for example, when she returned to her hutch to recharge her batteries. He also suggested that the machines did more than model animal-like behaviour and he assigned mental states and personalities to them:

> Elsie was afflicted with a very unstable, very feminine mode; her regulating mechanism was hypersensitive . . . as a result she very

quickly ran down her batteries running hither and thither to find an ideal condition. Elmer on the other hand had been given a very stable, very bourgeois character . . . But Grey Walter said: 'His reflexes are really lacking, he is quite lifeless. For days on end he doesn't stir from under the furniture; I must liven him up a bit and make him more intelligent. Because, you see, if an individual is intelligent he has to pay the price of a certain amount of accompanying irritability. Thus our radio sets, when they are too finely tuned suffer from a certain amount of instability.'[33]

The association between gender, irritability, sensitivity, intelligence and even psychiatric illness may seem curiously literal, but it is a familiar trope in the early years of cybernetics. Nowadays, electronic equipment is highly stable and self-correcting, but wartime experimenters had spent years in an electronic arms race, battling to produce equipment with higher power and shorter wavelengths and pushing the art of electronics to the limit of what was achievable.[34] Members of the Ratio Club would have been highly familiar with the ailments and instabilities of complex electronic devices and so the metaphor must have seemed, at that time, remarkably appropriate. Nevertheless, it is a curious formulation, both flattering and excusing a highly tuned and intelligent thinker like, perhaps, Grey Walter himself.

W. ROSS ASHBY AND THE HOMEOSTAT

Grey Walter's tortoises were clearly intended to persuade us to a mechanistic view of intelligence. His arguments about the nature of mentality and the closeness to which his creations approached artificial life were reinforced by the language he used to describe them, by giving them Cod Latin Linnaean species names (*Machina speculatrix*), and by suggesting a direct equivalence between his machines and his young son Timothy, whose birth he referred to as 'the delivery of a male homeostat which I . . . [am] anxious to get into commission as soon as possible'.[35]

But while Walter's tortoises were achieving remarkable celebrity, a quite different type of lifelike machine was built, intriguingly, in the same institution, Barnwood House, Gloucester, by Walter's colleague and fellow pioneer of cybernetics, the psychiatrist W. Ross Ashby, director of research there from 1947 to 1959.

In contrast to the theatricality of the 'tortoise show', Ashby's 'homeostat' was an understated cybernetic device of great subtlety that could probably only be properly appreciated by those who were literate in electronics. The homeostat was designed to emulate life by maintaining its own equilibrium in spite of external challenges and changes of conditions. In a curious way these devices – tortoise and homeostat – mirrored the character of each inventor. The tortoises were surprising and demanded attention. The homeostat seemed to reflect Ashby's altogether more reticent and typically academic personality. It was a rather obscure assembly of electronic components, culled, as was usual at the time, from war-surplus electronics shops and consisting of

The homeostat
of W. Ross Ashby.

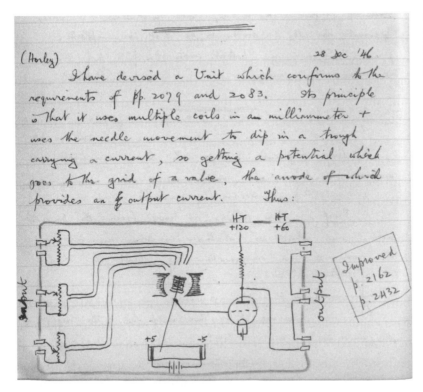

(Horley)   28 Dec '46

I have devised a Unit which conforms to the requirements of pp. 2079 and 2083. Its principle is that it uses multiple coils in an milliammeter + uses the needle movement to dip in a trough carrying a current, so getting a potential which goes to the grid of a valve, the anode of which provides an & output current.   Thus:

Original sketch of the circuitry of the homeostat, entry from Ross Ashby's notebook for 28 December 1946.

four electronic subunits (reputedly ex-RAF bomb control switchgear), each surmounted by a swivelling magnet that constituted the 'output' or display. These magnets aligned themselves like compass needles in a particular direction under the influence of coil electromagnets.

Visitors were invited to provoke the machine by switching electrical resistances in or out of circuit, changing or even reversing voltages and so on, on one or other of the subunits. After some brief gyrations, the electromagnet on the unit in question invariably seemed to settle down again to its proper place, and the others made tiny sympathetic movements. It seemed that the other three interlinked units conspired to stabilize the one that had been assaulted by the experimenter.

It is quite hard, now, to understand why the machine seemed quite so exciting when, in fact, it did so little, but it struck a chord with biologists because homeostasis – self-regulation – was a key concept in physiology and was seen as an essential property of life.

Non-scientists would certainly have needed an exposition from the inventor in order to appreciate the potential of the machine but went away entirely convinced by the insights that it provided. Radar and electronics people who had spent the Second World War wrestling with the endemic instability of their circuits found the stability of the homeostat equally magical. The *Daily Herald* newspaper, for example, headed an article on the homeostat with the hyperbolic claim that Ashby's 'Clicking brain is cleverer than man's'.[36] For Norbert Wiener, with his commitment to a new experimental philosophy relying on cybernetics and hardware, the homeostat was 'one of the great philosophical contributions of the present day'.[37]

CYBERNETICS AND PSYCHIATRY

Both Ashby and Grey Walter were professionally associated with Barnwood House, near Bristol, founded as a private mental hospital in the nineteenth century. It was here that German psychiatrist Lothar Kalinowsky, who had seen electroconvulsive therapy (ECT) in Rome with its originator Ugo Cerletti, demonstrated it on five patients in 1939. This led to the first published report on ECT in England and Grey Walter was closely involved.[38]

So ECT treatment pre-dated cybernetics, but it soon appeared to be a thoroughly cybernetic treatment. Indeed, cybernetics seemed to offer a justification for it and for other techniques involved at the time used in the 'the heroic treatment of mental illness'. In his book, under the heading 'Cybernetics and Psychopathology', Norbert Wiener suggested that 'the realization that the brain and the computing machine have much in common may suggest new and valid approaches to psychopathology, and even to psychiatrics.'[39]

He mused that 'psychopathology has been rather a disappointment to the instinctive materialism of the doctors', since no structural or histological changes could be found in most psychiatric conditions. 'There is no way of identifying the brain of a schizophrenic . . . Nor of a manic depressive, nor of a paranoiac.'

This was because, Wiener suggested, 'it is not the empty physical structure of the computing machine that corresponds to the brain . . . but the combination of this structure with the instructions given to it . . . and . . . the additional information stored and gained from outside.' Psychiatric problems, he argued, were primarily software problems (to use a term that arrived a little later in computing) and Wiener suggested that in the brain, 'the instructions' were stored in the form of 'circulating memories with a physical basis which vanishes when the machine is shut down'. This is a close analogy with early computer memory systems like acoustic mercury delay lines and cathode ray tube memory storage (the Williams Tube), which were active, electronic repeating systems. Mental disorders, he suggested, were diseases of memory, in which bad or 'specious' memories – neurotic worries – continued to circulate and involve an increasing number of neurons so that 'it is possible that the patient simply does not have room, the sufficient number of neurons, to carry out his normal processes of thought.'[40]

And so psychiatric treatment could be analogous to the mechanistic, ad hoc tricks used to fix the glitches in the electronic machines that he was familiar with – the radar sets and computers used in anti-aircraft gunnery:

The first thing which we try is to clear the machine of all information, [by switching it off] in the hope that when it starts again with different data the difficulty may not recur. Failing this . . . we shake the machine, or, if it is electrical, subject it to an abnormally large electrical impulse in the hope that we may reach the inaccessible part and throw it into a position where the false cycle of its activities will be interrupted.

For Wiener, the various forms of shock treatment then used in psychiatric care, including drug-induced comas with insulin, metrazol and with electric shock therapy itself, were all seen as ways of 'shaking the machine . . . violent, imperfectly understood, imperfectly controlled method[s] to interrupt a mental vicious cycle'.[41]

Ross Ashby did not make so simplistic a comparison between machine circuitry and the brain, although he did discuss 'switching the machine off and starting again', or subjecting the machine to 'a brief but maximal electrical impulse'.[42] But, for him, the greater challenge was the property of stability, which he had modelled in the homeostat as the essential characteristic of living things. Treatment to him seemed to be a contest between two stable entities: 'an imposition of the therapist's will on the patient's; it is therefore a form of war'. He wrote in his personal journal of what he called 'Blitz treatment', using techniques like ECT, hypnosis and LSD drug treatments in combination: 'hitting hard & seeing what happens'.[43]

WORLD MACHINES AND 'GOVERNMENT MACHINES'

For a while cybernetics was enormously influential, seeming to fulfil the hopes of Wiener and others for a revolution in psychiatry, the science of mind and consciousness, and as a way to understand social organizations, businesses and politics of nations. In this spirit Ross Ashby saw beyond his 'homeostat' to 'machine government', where a 'Solomon-like computer' would replace squabbling politicians to make rational, and therefore generally acceptable, decisions: 'The machine of the future, says Ashby, will be able to explore domains far too complex and far too subtle to be envisaged by human intelligence.'[44]

Ashby's world government machine would be fed enormous tables of statistics and masses of scientific facts: 'Mankind would have to obey the new Sybils blindly, without attempting to understand them, and little by little it would see its difficulties vanishing . . . the machines will govern the experts who made them and the experts will govern the masses in the name of the sacrosanct and infallible machines.'[45]

Ashby saw the trajectory of computation perhaps even more clearly than his colleagues in computing science, envisaging real artificial intelligence (AI) and 'the intelligent machine' that would solve the economic and political problems 'which often baffle the expert':

For example, in order to fix the price of butter, the authorities have to consider a number of things: the net cost, the volume of productivity, the purchasing power of the consumer, the policy of the producers, the wholesalers, the retailers, the demands of political parties and trade unions, the requirements of international markets etc. [Such a machine] would certainly make as good a job of it as the bureaucrats.[46]

After the futurism of the world government machine, this 'butter machine' seems to have a remarkably humble duty for what would have been one of the latest and most complex computers yet made. Yet it is an insight into the milieu of this cybernetic work for the butter machine is securely located in the administrative habits of the immediate post-war world. Britain had run the war with the most meticulous government systems for planning and for the production and supply of virtually every article. It was a planning regime so extensive that, A.J.P. Taylor boasted, it surpassed anything seen in Soviet Russia and in post-war Britain much of this planning apparatus survived to be used by both Labour and Conservative governments. There was a government Egg Marketing Board, a Potato Marketing Board and a Milk Marketing Board, which did, in fact, have the job of regulating the price of butter, although not by computer.[47]

However, a 'government machine', of a kind, was eventually made. Stafford Beer, perhaps the most influential second-generation British cybernetician, networked Chile in 1972 with a computer information system he called 'Cybersyn' to run production and distribution across the country.[48] With the overthrow and death of Salvador Allende, Cybersyn was dismantled. The new right-wing military government of Augusto Pinochet did not, it seems, realize how useful the integrated information system it had inherited could be.

Stafford Beer had long been a celebrity cybernetician and management consultant, best known for his 1972 work *The Brain of the Firm*, which used the human nervous system as a model for human social organizations, companies or governments. He had been thinking

Stafford Beer as celebrity management consultant for SIGMA, the firm he helped found in 1961.

about the diffused intelligence that permeated organizations for a long time before his Chilean adventure.

In 1964 Gerald Leach, at the BBC, speculated about scientific ideas that would make good subjects for the new BBC science programme *Monitor*. He noted that

> Operational Research [O.R.] was enormously successful during the war. Fifteen years later, backed by their computers, the O.R. boys are now saying that they and their computers could take over from the politicians. (Stafford Beer recently approached the Ministry for Science with a complete plan for running the country which excluded politicians entirely – or so I am told by the Ministry.) How would Beer do it? And a reply from a Cabinet Minister.[49]

The programme was never made.

THE MECHANIZATION OF THOUGHT

In Britain, one effect of the cybernetics movement was to make the notion of artificial intelligence seem familiar and even probable. In 1958 the National Physical Laboratory hosted a symposium. Its title, 'The Mechanisation of Thought Processes', is emblematic of the spirit of the times and of its optimism and energy. The event attracted many members of the Ratio Club, but also delegates from the USA and Soviet Russia. The speakers included Ross Ashby, Warren McCulloch and many future stars of the artificial intelligence world including, from MIT, Marvin Minsky, John McCarthy and Oliver Selfridge.

One of the most significant developments in Britain, in the years following the NPL symposium, was the establishment of a school of machine intelligence at the University of Edinburgh. The department was started by Donald Michie, the brilliant polymath and computer scientist whose first 'university' had been the Bletchley Park cryptographic centre, which he joined straight from school during the Second World War.

A major project of the group was the design of the robot that they named Freddy, a machine that was designed to recognize and assemble parts jumbled at random on a tabletop. For experimental development the components of a simple model boat and a model car were used, but Freddy was meant to lead on to more universal robots for handling and assembly tasks that would have the power to recognize complex parts in an industrial setting, whichever way up they were, and assemble them in the correct order and orientation.

By 1970 Freddy could assemble the models in about sixteen hours, which required continuous operation of the Elliott 4130 computer for

The Freddy robot had binocular vision for depth perception and a pincer hand to pick and place parts. Freddy II, a later model, shown here, is today on display at the National Museum of Scotland.

the whole duration. Although a human five-year-old could probably have done the task in half an hour or so, it was still an extraordinary achievement and helped to illustrate a crucial problem in artificial intelligence. How much does the machine have to 'know' to function in the world? These first experiments quickly showed the challenges of getting robots, even with a good binocular vision system, to recognize objects, whatever their orientation. There are so many cues that humans use that are unconsciously adopted, and so much that has already been learned throughout life about the physical world. AI experimenters were rediscovering Kenneth Craik's view that acting in the world required the construction of a mental model of it.[50] The hard part was the realization that the new electronic brain needs to know an awful lot and these sixteen-hour computer runs in Edinburgh 'raised the interesting question of whether this was an unavoidably hard problem which simply needed very much more powerful computers, or whether there was another computationally cheaper way of tackling the problem'.[51] The spirit of cybernetics implied that machine developers could do this by the thoughtful analysis of human and animal behaviour. Grey Walter's tortoises had quite simple circuitry but generated surprising behaviour. Weren't they clues to modelling complex attributes like perception, decision and performance?

An example of this episodic but exhilarating approach was the problem delineated by Jack Good in a lecture given at the department in Edinburgh around 1972. Good, one of the post-war pioneers of artificial intelligence (and, like Michie, a former code-breaker from Bletchley Park), gave the illuminating example of a fielder catching a ball in a game of cricket (or baseball). He set out what a formal computer-directed machine would need to measure and calculate to be in the right place as the ball descended. It must repeatedly measure speed and position to compute the deceleration of the ball, its trajectory and the place at which it will arrive, while some interlinked calculations about the fielder's own motion and acceleration are also needed. The human fielder does not do anything so difficult, Good argued, for there is a simple rule: 'If the ball appears to rise in the sky, run backwards.

If it is falling, run towards it.' Armed with this algorithm, Good's hypothetical robot cricket fielder should arrive at the right spot but, unlike a rigorous control program, it has no internal representation of real physical laws: it does not 'know', or have to know, Newton's laws of motion.[52]

This is a striking example of the strengths and deficiencies of the cybernetic approach. It was insightful, seductive and capable of suggesting breathtaking short cuts. In the emerging world of mainframe computers, with their laboriously written, long programs and all-night

Fred Ordway (left) and Jack Good (right) on the set of *2001: A Space Odyssey* in Hertfordshire, England, March 1966. Good acted as scientific advisor to Stanley Kubrick during filming.

runs, insights like this were thought-provoking and encouraging, but perhaps – to some – a little too flashy.

This approach epitomized what has come to be called 'scruffy', as opposed to the 'neat' school of AI. 'Neats' wanted the programming solutions to be explicit and mathematically rigorous. (The dichotomy has also been characterized as 'pious' or 'naughty'.) 'Scruffies' wanted to try many things, write and observe experimental programs and to adjust and hack them until they began to perform right. In their formulation, there was simply too much to know about intelligent performances to wait to construct formal solutions. The cricket fielder was a perfect example of the scruffy approach.[53]

Of course there was much that Good ignored and, though the visual cue of the ball appearing to rise or fall seems to be one that we do use, he did not discuss all the other anticipations we make in the course of that apparently simple act of catching, not least those few milliseconds of pure extrapolation when the ball passes out of the field of direct vision. How does he then extend a hand so accurately for the intuitive catch high above his head, or at knee height?

This thought experiment could serve as parable for the dawning realization of the deep intractability and the mystery of human (and animal) performance for nothing about acting in the real world is simple. The 'scruffy and neat' dichotomy has faded, since most approaches now need to use both: a combination of expediency, inspiration and theoretical insight. But there is still no robot cricket catcher, and, when we try to emulate these reactive responses by machine, human performances seem so complex and so wonderful that the neurophilosopher Patricia Churchland has described them as 'every bit as mysterious . . . as consciousness itself'.[54]

And so, Good's cricketer, in retrospect, seems to lead to the sense that there was no real systematic cybernetic science but only special insights generated by a peculiarly creative and original group of people. As it turned out, the pursuit of lifelike, or at least intelligent and reactive, behaviour turned up many problems that were not susceptible to this type of short cut. For example, the Freddy robot needed to be able to recognize the parts it was looking at whatever way up they were.[55] It also needed, of course, to 'know' what the finished results – the car and the boat – should be like. And Freddy required a 'geometry', a set of spatial rules, to make sense of its tabletop world and for the recognition and the correct reorientation and alignment of all the parts.

Freddy had taken the researchers into a new world of pattern recognition and of modelling its world – quite close, it seems, to an older world of philosophical speculation about the senses. Real, self-directing robots, it seemed, would have to relearn or re-enact the model-making, perceptions, judgements and learning that intelligent creatures deploy (and how hard it has turned out to be). In this magnificently complex and challenging new world of intellectual endeavour there were just too few brilliant short cuts like Jack Good's fielder to produce the rapid results that AI enthusiasts hoped for, and the sceptics were about to forcefully point this out.

THE LIGHTHILL REPORT

By the early 1970s the Science Research Council in Britain started to become concerned by the number of funding requests it was receiving from the various artificial intelligence and computer science groups and commissioned a report from Sir James Lighthill, an applied mathematician and former director of the Royal Aircraft Establishment at Farnborough. At the time, the Edinburgh group wanted funding to buy a much more powerful state-of-the-art computer.

Lighthill approached the field of AI research with deep scepticism, perhaps influenced by the philosopher Hubert Dreyfus and his highly contentious 1965 paper 'Alchemy and AI'. Dreyfus, based at MIT, had been commissioned by the RAND Corporation in the USA to review the topic. His report, when released, proved to be a bombshell. For Dreyfus, AI was notable for its false claims and undue optimism. Thought was not the same as computation, humans had properties like 'ambiguity tolerance' and unconscious instincts, and mental processes were not like, and could not be modelled by, formal digital, symbolic manipulations.

Neurones were not 'on-off' devices (as McCulloch had argued) but had complex analogue states. Acting in the world was immensely subtle and Drexler's view of it was more attuned to Heidegger's phenomenology and his philosophy of mind. Drexler's approach was inherently at odds with the mechanistic and reductionist world of the AI practitioners.[56]

Back in the UK, Lighthill delivered a report in 1972 that was also highly sceptical of the prospects for AI and robotics. Like Dreyfus, he considered that the practitioners of the discipline had consistently overpromised and underdelivered. He observed that 'the difficulty of achieving good hand-eye coordination in quite simple problem situations has proved unexpectedly great,' and reflected that work to date 'seems to hold out negligible hope of approaching human levels of achievement'. The robotic assembly performance of Freddy impressed him not at all, because he believed that the film he had been shown of Freddy at work, apparently doing a seamless job of construction, was sleight of hand, edited together from separate short sequences of Freddy accomplishing different phases of the job.

Lighthill seemed to think that Donald Michie and his team had wilfully 'put one over him'. The whole field was bedevilled with grandiose claims, thought Lighthill, reflecting that while academic groups were wrestling with high-level and intractable issues of pattern recognition and spatial modelling, the pragmatic control engineers from industry were, meanwhile, delivering practical machines for assembly and mechanical handling that owed nothing to theoretical pretensions. Furthermore, the new Smiths Industries auto-landing system for aircraft had ability of a higher level: it was a highly robust computer-based system replicating a difficult human skill, which owed everything to industrial development engineers and nothing at all to academic AI research.

In the following year, Lighthill engaged with many of the prominent members of the AI community (perhaps unwisely for them) in a debate at the Royal Institution. In fact, it was less a debate than a kind of Soviet show trial, where Lighthill took centre stage and heaped scorn on the whole field of AI, on poor Freddy, and on his achievements. Declining to see Freddy as a brave, but preliminary, model system, he argued that his successes at assembling models could only be accomplished in the grossly simplified environment that had been constructed for him, what Lighthill called 'a playpen world'. Freddy might be 'an ingenious product of computer science', but no more.

For a real general-purpose robot to become a reality, Lighthill argued, it would have to be able to tackle new problems not expected by the programmer, but, he argued, as the experimental tasks and events became more realistic and more complicated, the variables, and their interactions, would multiply startlingly and would pose an intractable computational problem. The roadblock, in his view, would be an insuperable mathematical quagmire that he termed a 'combinatorial explosion', and so 'the general-purpose robot is a mirage.'[57]

ARTIFICIAL INTELLIGENCE AND THE AFTERLIFE OF CYBERNETICS

In Britain the Lighthill affair seemed to signal the start of the 'AI winter', a period when research funds were choked off. Something similar also happened in the USA, perhaps triggered by the failure of the machine translation project, a cherished Cold War baby that Dreyfus had singled out for particular disdain in his 1965 RAND paper.

But what of cybernetics itself? As a 'theory of everything' from neurology to politics, cybernetics seemed to pale as a subject. In retrospect it seems now more like a movement than a coherent scientific discipline and by the late 1970s most centres for it had 'died of dry rot'.[58] Cybernetics did not achieve the status of a mainstream academic subject, leaving behind the impression that it was more a movement than a science fuelled by the personal insights of a cadre of exceptionally talented and resourceful people. Perhaps it was simply the short-lived artefact of a highly technical war, a scientific pressure cooker that had given this group of talented and resourceful scientists a unique cross-disciplinary experience.

The main stars of the field also gradually dropped away. Norbert Wiener died in 1964, although Warren McCulloch was actively teaching

Ross Ashby
at Stanford University,
December 1955.

and debating up to his death in 1969. In Britain, as chance had it, Ross Ashby was, in fact, Grey Walter's boss at Barnwood House. According to legend, he arranged for Grey Walter to be followed by private detectives, perhaps out of impatience with Grey's notoriously louche lifestyle. These events, combined with other ill-chosen administrative decisions, encouraged him to leave Britain for the USA. Meanwhile, back in Bristol, Grey Walter's active research career was brought to a close by an unusual event that does not seem so extraordinary in the context of his whole life, for he collided with a runaway horse while riding his motor scooter.[59] Stafford Beer, partly disillusioned by his experiences in Chile, retired from industrial work and cybernetics to rural Wales, where he became a practitioner of tantric yoga.

The loss of all these outstanding figures clearly weakened the status of cybernetics. Nevertheless, departments of artificial intelligence and robotics, subjects which had largely originated within cybernetics, continued to multiply, perhaps because they had clearer and more specific goals.

Today robots are everywhere, but the industrial machines used in production for handling, welding, assembly and painting are very far from the devices that artificial intelligence researchers expected we would have by now: 'real robots' that could substitute for a human over a wide range of human activities.

This is, in part, because giving robots the symbolic models of the world that are needed has proved amazingly hard. There is so much that needs to be known about so many things, and also almost everything in the world is semantically unstable. A pile of bricks implies one thing on a building site and something quite different when encountered by a rioting crowd. Almost anything can migrate from utility to threat but may also move in almost any other practical or emotional direction, a challenge that AI researchers refer to as 'the frame problem'. All this seems quite obvious when we reflect on the way that humans perform, for we have all experienced the long and intricate process of programming called 'growing up'. Seen in this light, seemingly trivial events, such as a baby's habit of persistently pushing its cup or a biscuit off the edge of its tray, can be seen as a learning experiment that reveals practical truths about the geometry of the world and about gravity ('Where does it go?'). The problems of replicating human performances have demonstrated that real, flexible and multivalent artificial intelligence is strikingly elusive. As AI researchers like Alan Winfield, one of the founders of the Bristol Robotics Laboratory, have mused, 'the things that looked to be hard, in the post-war world, like chess, have proved to be (relatively) simple. The things that might, at first sight, have seemed easy for a machine, like making a cup of tea in someone else's kitchen, have proved, so far, to be insuperably hard.'[60]

Robots represent a subset of the whole problem of artificial intelligence. Today, the rhetoric around AI is so fevered that it seems foolhardy to say, with Lighthill and perhaps with Dreyfus, that both robots and

Robot painters at Ferrari. In spite of their balletic movements, contemporary automata used across the car industry are entirely deterministic, using electronics rather than the pinwheels and cams that made 18th-century automata like Vaucanson's flute-player seem so extraordinary.

AI are still mirages. The self-driving car is often seen as the key test for AI in the early twenty-first century and is almost here, its boosters claim. So far its progress is looking dicey. Will it really interact with free-flowing mixed traffic, where thousands of drivers and riders signal and detect intentions almost subliminally and, generally, collaborate in split-second decision making?

The paradox is that Grey Walter's 1950s tortoises showed intriguingly lifelike behaviour from a simple circuit with few sensors and simple components, but today even the best research robots, equipped with vastly greater computing power, memory and dedicated programming, remind us of their mechanical natures with almost every step or gesture. It seems that our expectations of cybernetic or robotic performances continually increase: for although celebrity robots like Asimo or Robo-Thespian represent an extraordinary feat of engineering development and programming, we now study their every robot response intently for signs of unnaturalness.

The anticipated convergence between human activity and mechanized thought has not occurred. Brain events remain deeply obscure and Walter McCulloch's hypothetical 1964 psychon – his proposition of the single, simplest, atomistic mental event – has not been discovered. While there are many intriguing studies of the active brains of humans

Sophia, famous for being the first robot to achieve formal citizenship, in 2017, communicates in scripted soundbites evidently constructed to promote the AI movement.

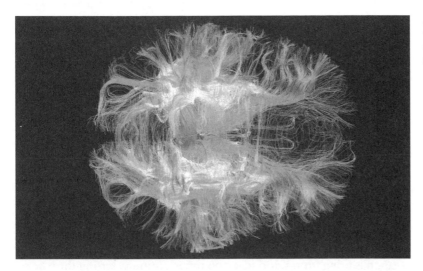

A current connectomics visualization. But how are experiences, memories and intentions encoded?

using magnetic resonance imaging, these generally show only what areas of the brain appear to be metabolically active or areas that seem to be in collaborative relationships at particular times. They give no hint as what form the actual 'signals traffic' takes. Perhaps for this reason hopes have begun to rest on connectomics, the detailed micro-anatomy of the brain. If the full wiring diagram of every neurone and its connections could be mapped and emulated on a machine, wouldn't this recreate the functionality of the particular brain that had been mapped?

Again though, whatever the anatomical interest of this work, the enterprise does not seem to hold out much hope for understanding the neural electrical traffic itself or the coding form that memory, emotion, pain or action take.

So where does real AI flourish at its most responsive, reactive and most autonomous? One answer must be in air defence – where it started. Tactical anti-missile systems of the type developed to counter surface-skimming missiles like the notorious Exocet can be operated in fully autonomous mode, particularly on board warships. These systems analyse the flight path, speed, heading and radar signature of the suspect target and, if it fulfils the criteria established for a threat, destroy it. Of course, awful mistakes must occur. These systems can be set to give an alarm and wait for human instructions but in hostile environments there may not be time to consult. These defensive weapon systems have a built-in setting for fully autonomous operation.

The most impressive examples of this kind of smart air defence are the current anti-aircraft gun sets like the American Phalanx close-in weapon system or the European Rheinmetall Oerlikon Millennium Gun. Though military hardware specialists tend to regard AA guns nowadays as second best to missiles, perhaps because they are cheaper, these are the defensive weapons of last resort and in computational terms the job they do is astounding. They track the target and discard all the jamming and decoy information while calculating the aiming lead for the weapon. And then they construct a cloud of shell bursts around the target: every shot is aimed with micrometer adjustment even though the weapon is firing from 1,000 to 4,000 times a minute, setting the fuse on the shell electronically as it passes up the barrel and even measuring and adjusting for increasing muzzle velocity as the gun heats up during the burst. The job these systems are designed for is highly defined and limited, and within this task-specific arena these guns are intelligent.

While politicians and ethicists debate the morality, and the imminent prospect of, robotized weapon systems, these air defence gun sets are already in service. They come supplied with the optional choice of human control or fully autonomous operation – it is just the flick of a switch.

6

COWBOYS, COLTS
AND KALASHNIKOVS

Until a few years ago the Lakota 'ghost shirt', a mysterious and emotive object that came from the massacre at Wounded Knee in 1890, could be seen at the Kelvingrove Art Gallery and Museum, Glasgow. Embroidered and tasselled, it is an ochre colour stained, in patches, a rusty red. The owner was almost certainly killed in it.

The new Ghost Dance religion had been developing in the 1890s and spread among some of the Native American peoples as their treaties with the u.s. government were dishonoured and they were forced onto ever more marginal land by the endless tide of European settlement. The religion seems to have adopted elements of Native American beliefs, but also some from Christianity, promising salvation not from sin, but from oppression.[1] The white men would be driven out, the Indians would recover their lands, the buffalo would return. Believers expected immunity from bullets through ritual clothing – the Ghost Shirts – and the sacred Ghost Dance.

The last act in this flickering and almost extinguished nationalism was played out in a desolate stretch of South Dakota to where the Lakota, a branch of the Sioux, had camped, harassed by the army and worn down by crop failure and the virtual extinction of the buffalo.[2] There the army began a search to disarm them. One Lakota, it seems, fired his rifle, prompting a torrent of fire from a hostile and nervous army. The result was an appalling massacre, not only of armed men, but of women and children, shot down as they fled. The great chief, Sitting Bull, is said to have been killed in his tent, where he lay desperately

The 'Glasgow' Lakota
ghost shirt from
Wounded Knee at the
Kelvingrove Museum
in 1998. Glasgow City
Council agreed to
return it in 1999 to
the Wounded Knee
Survivors Association.

ill with pneumonia. At the time the shooting broke out he had been engaged in a parlay with the army officers.

It is significant that the soldiers were from the 7th Cavalry, the regiment that had fielded the force under General Custer that had been destroyed fourteen years before at the Battle of Little Bighorn. There, an association of Lakota, northern Cheyenne and Arapaho had encountered Custer's men and wiped them out, killing some 270 men with virtually no survivors. Custer's management of the earlier battle remains a mystery, for given the right tactics and disciplined fire, the cavalry should have been able to hold off the foe, but the defensive enclaves they established were encircled, weakened and then overwhelmed 'in less time than it takes a hungry man to eat a meal'.[3] It has been suggested that the cavalry was outgunned because, on that occasion, they had, for the most part, Colt revolvers and single-shot Springfield rifles. The Indian alliance had a large range of weapons including bows and arrows, Colts as well, antique single-shot muskets, but also a good number of rapid-fire repeating Winchester magazine rifles. The cavalry's Springfields, however, were capable of sustained and accurate fire in well-trained hands. Perhaps that was the problem, because the value of marksmanship had been little appreciated in the army until then: the yearly allowance for practice was said to be a mere twenty cartridges a year. By contrast the Native Americans were expert shots, intensely skilled at hunting and at handling their arms.

The disparity between the opponents, perhaps, was similar to the shock that the British army encountered in the Boer War. The British army was trained by careful drill to lay down intense and sustained fire from lines of soldiers, firing and reloading in relays, though at comparatively short range (perhaps 200 yards or less), the technique that the army still called 'musketry'. The weapons were not particularly accurate and in earlier European conflicts volume of fire had been the main point: marksmanship had not been a priority. The Boers, however, avoided this kind of head to head slaughter. Brought up as resourceful farmers and hunters, they were crack shots and had new, long-range and more accurate rifles, mostly German-made Mausers, with which they could strike lethally from well outside the range of British fire.

In any case, the cavalry took no chances at Wounded Knee. The mission was to disarm the Lakota and they surrounded the Lakota camp, also deploying four Hotchkiss 'mountain guns', small cannon firing canisters of grapeshot.[4] The firepower was overwhelming and, quite unlike the earlier encounter with Custer, the Lakota were not mounted and drawn up ready to fight but dispirited, hungry and,

Photographs at Wounded Knee a few days after the massacre, with some of the dead, including Chief Big Foot, frozen in the snow. Opposite: 'Gathering the Dead' (top), and 'Burial of the Dead' (bottom).

apparently, on their way to surrender. This time the Native Americans were heavily outgunned.

A few days after the killing, some of the three hundred Lakota corpses frozen and stiff in the thin snow, were photographed, almost casually, by George Trager, who had travelled from his studio about 80 km (50 mi.) away in Nebraska. The Glasgow ghost shirt, it is said, was

The loss of the buffalo: a pile of buffalo skulls. At first, the purpose of systematic buffalo hunting was to feed the large crews of navvies building the new railroads across the American continent. Later it became a sport, and then, by the 1870s, a mission to exterminate the herds and starve the Plains Indians who depended on them into submission. There was even a slogan: 'one less buffalo means one less Indian.'

recovered there, possibly by Short Bull, who had blessed it before the encounter. Indeed, Short Bull, with Kicking Bear, had brought the religion back from Nevada after visiting Wovoka, the messianic visionary of the Paiute people and part-founder of the religion.

Years later, Black Elk, a medicine man of the Lakota people, recalled:

I did not know then how much was ended. When I look back now from this high hill of my old age, I can still see the butchered women and children lying heaped and scattered all along the crooked gulch as plain as when I saw them with eyes young. And I can see that something else died there in the bloody mud and was buried in the blizzard. A people's dream died there. It was a beautiful dream . . . the nation's hoop is broken and scattered. There is no center any longer, and the sacred tree is dead.[5]

Perhaps the final outcome for the Native Americans was a historical inevitability, brought about by European immigration, the steamship, the railway, the growing power of the u.s. Army and its weaponry. But there were other weapons that the Native Americans did not have. They did not have title deeds or property registers. They did not have lawyers.

Some of the Lakota, the ones thought most likely to lead further insurrections, were imprisoned at the u.s. Army post at Fort Sheridan, Illinois. However, Short Bull was released, along with several other Lakota prisoners, on Buffalo Bill Cody's surety, to join his Wild West show. This was not such a strange decision, for the travelling show took them far from their settlements and their peoples and, although they displayed on stage their warlike skills and horsemanship, the cowboys always won.

Buffalo Bill Cody's spectacular show was highly successful, at first touring the East Coast and the more settled regions of America. Indeed, one of the extraordinary twists of the story is that cowboy shows had been popular for a long time and Indians had been appearing in performance, even while their own compatriots and relatives were still fighting settlers and the military in the West. Cody also brought his show to Great Britain three times and in 1892 played at fourteen venues including Leeds, Liverpool, Manchester, Brighton, Bristol and London.

Albert Berghaus, 'The Far West: Shooting Buffalo on the Line of the Kansas–Pacific Railroad', engraving from *Frank Leslie's Illustrated Newspaper* (3 June 1871).

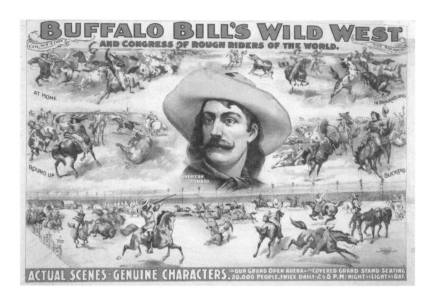

Poster for Buffalo Bill's Wild West show (top) and a studio shot of some of the members, including Short Bull, top left.

Colt model 1873
Single Action Army
revolver owned
by William F.
'Buffalo Bill' Cody.

By one of those strange turns, we meet again here Admiral Lord
Charles Beresford, fierce foe of Jacky Fisher at the head of the Royal
Navy, and the nemesis, almost, of reforming gunnery expert Admiral Sir
Percy Scott. An Anglo-Irish peer, Beresford was a fearless rider, obsessed
with horsemanship and hunting, having, according to legend, a florid
fox-hunting scene tattooed across his posterior. When Buffalo Bill came
to London, Beresford, it seems, was fascinated by the unfamiliar and
distinct styles of horsemanship displayed by the cowboys and by the
Indians and somehow got in touch with Cody for a closer look. He
emerged before the public ensconced in the Deadwood Stage in a famous
scene in the show where the stagecoach was galloped around the arena,
with mounted Indian braves in pursuit, howling bloodthirsty cries.[6]

The best reception for Cody's show in Britain, however, was in
Glasgow, for perhaps the fate of the Indians evoked memories of the
Highland Clearances. The scenes seemed to have extraordinary resonance

in Scotland and the group played there for a month at the East End exhibition centre in Dennistoun. Thousands saw the performances and the entourage became famous in the town with Cody attending a football match at Ibrox between Celtic and Dumbarton, where his imposing figure, fabulous attire and tall white cowboy hat created huge interest. (He arrived late to enhance the dramatic effect.)

The theme of Cody's Wild West show was epitomized by its title, *The Drama of Civilisation*, seemingly a rather slender dramatic vehicle that loosely held together its essential appeal: the fabulous displays of horse riding, sharp-shooting, including the crack shot Annie Oakley, and what was perhaps the most exotic element – the handsome Lakota with their proud bearing.

The episodes in the drama included attacks on waggon trains, attacks on ranches with the Indians being ridden down or shot by the cowboys, and, of course, the pursuit of the Deadwood Stage. These gripping sequences of cowboy and Indian encounters were firmly established by Cody (and by various imitators) long before Hollywood came to recognize them as invaluable dramatic tropes.[7]

At the end of the run, and before the troupe embarked for America, George Crager, who was travelling with the show as Lakota interpreter, arranged for the Kelvingrove Museum to acquire 31 Lakota items. The collection included the Ghost Shirt, a ceremonial necklace of grizzly bear claws worn by Short Bull when he brought back the Ghost Dance religion from Nevada, and a beaded buckskin waistcoat worn by Rain in the Face at Little Bighorn. Surprisingly, since Crager has been described as 'a chancer', he sold only fifteen of the items and donated the rest. Could it be that the Lakota in the troupe objected to the sale of the more sensitive items? Curiously, on that tour, one of the Lakota, Charging Thunder, was imprisoned in Barlinnie Gaol for thirty days after assaulting Crager with an Indian club. It was said at his trial that he was generally the most peaceable of the Indians and bore Crager no malice, but had been drinking whisky.

And what of Short Bull, also travelling with the show? How, one wonders, did he bear his own trajectory from warrior-priest to 'stage

Sitting Bull and William F. 'Buffalo Bill' Cody, August 1885. Mutual respect or cynical stunt?

Indian'? But the actions of our ancestors in the past, and the relationships, are more complicated than the histories often allow. Cody had respect for the Indians and, when he had grown famous, argued for fairer treatment for them. He was also a supporter of women's suffrage. He described the great Lakota chief Sitting Bull, the victor of Little Bighorn, as a friend and travelled to Standing Rock in the Dakota territory, where the Indian Police – government agents – were trying to arrest him to end Lakota resistance and to suppress the Ghost Dance. Cody hoped to mediate and avoid a stand-off, but he was detained by other officers en route, plied with whisky, and arrived too late. Sitting Bull was killed, probably intentionally murdered, in a botched arrest.[8]

In 1999 the Lakota Wounded Knee Survivors Association requested the return of the shirt from Glasgow, arguing both that its original removal from the victim and from the battlefield was improper and illegal according to the laws of the time, but also on the basis of its importance as a sacred and culturally important relic. In a thoughtful paper for the hearing convened by Glasgow City Council on 13 November 1998, Mark O'Neill, head of Glasgow Museums, noted that although museums 'are temples of possession' and of preservation, there must be values that outweigh these ideals if museums also represent 'our better selves'. The decision was that Kelvingrove Art Gallery and Museum would return the relic to the Lakota people, the first cultural artefact to be returned to Native Americans by a British institution. It was replaced by a replica sewn by Marcella LeBeau, the granddaughter of Rain in the Face, who was at the killing grounds of both Little Bighorn and at Wounded Knee – a family closeness that demonstrates how near in memory to us historical tragedies really are.[9]

COLONEL COLT, THE REPEATING PISTOL AND THE WILD WEST

The American government experiment in the mass manufacture of guns, and the emerging East Coast armaments industry that resulted from it, made the gun an everyday object. The West was awash with guns and, as we saw, the Indians had firearms too of various types. But no one is so clearly identified with the arms of the West as Samuel Colt.

Samuel Colt was one of those inventive, bombastic Yankees with a genius for self-promotion, but also a very considerable talent for mechanism and machinery. In 1830, as a merchant seaman en route for India, he passed through London, seeing at first hand the works of some of the world's finest gunmakers in their showrooms. It is believed that he then saw a revolving pistol in a gun shop in Calcutta in 1831, 'an event so important that he deliberately lied about it in future years'. The weapon may have been a revolving flintlock pistol designed by his countryman Elisha Collier of Boston, who had travelled to Britain to patent it.[10]

As a 'natural-born Yankee', Colt had an inborn love of whittling wood, both as a pastime and to make useful items. According to legend, while he sailed home he carved a model revolver with his knife, a semi-functional wooden prototype showing his basic design and his innovation: the cylinder carrying the cartridges was rotated one step at each pull of the trigger to bring up a fresh round for the next shot. According to one account, Colt was impressed by the mechanism used for locking the ship's wheel in a single position, or perhaps it was the capstan winch for hauling in the anchor chain, which also had a sturdy pawl to lock it when needed.

Back in the USA Colt started manufacture of revolvers at Paterson, New Jersey, selling to the military, to individuals and for law enforcement. Soon he started using the style 'Colonel Colt', which was useful in dealing with official agencies. But though his detractors assumed that 'Colonel' was an honorific that he had awarded himself, it was, apparently, a legitimate title for he had been inducted into the Connecticut militia in 1850 by Thomas H. Seymour, whom Colt had helped to get elected as governor. Colt's chief function apparently was 'to make sure that Seymour got home not too drunk from official parties and receptions'.[11]

Colt began at a time when the new American government gunmaking processes, using gauges, standardization and repeatability, were becoming more widely known, and he seized these new production techniques. Indeed, his weapons became closely identified with the unstoppable power, accuracy and economy of this system. Even so, Colt was canny enough to know that true interchangeability, in which a part from any gun could replace its equivalent in any other, was at that time a luxury that only the military could pay for, given the natural error of available machine tools and the way dimensions could wander. He

therefore adopted an ingenious hybrid business strategy, selling 'perfect' weapons with carefully gauged interchangeable parts to the army, but rather than scrap the 'out of gauge' components, they were then selectively assembled into perfectly functional weapons for sale to the private market or small independent agencies.

There was, in fact, no reason why these hand-assembled weapons, which were built, in effect, on a variant of the British craft system, should be inferior, individually, to the special military selection, although it is said that a too casual exchange of parts between these second-line Colts could be dangerous. If, for example, the replacement cylinder was not a perfect fit, a sliver of lead could be shaved off the bullet as it was fired and blown out sideways between the cylinder and the barrel. It was possible, legend had it, for a bystander to be killed by a piece of this debris while standing alongside someone firing the weapon in another direction.

Samuel Colt, c. 1854. Colt's own flippant word on his invention, in a letter to Charles Manby, 18 May 1852, was that 'the good people of this world are very far from being satisfied with each other, and my arms are the best peacemakers.'

In 1851 Colt was back in London at the Great Exhibition in Hyde Park, where he took a stand to promote his wares and liberally dispensed brandy to potential clients and agents. Colt's entry in the exhibition catalogue anticipated a new 'Indian War' in America. He had recruited two former U.S. Army officers who provided a chilling and prophetic endorsement of Colt products. The entry quoted from a 'Report as to the Relative Efficiency of the Repeating Pistols' issued by the congressional Committee on Military Affairs:

> On the Texan frontier, and on the several routes to California, the Indian tribes are renewing their murderous warfare . . . General Harney, who employed Colt's pistol successfully in Florida [the war against the Seminoles] says 'it is the only weapon with which we can hope ever to subdue those wild and daring tribes.'

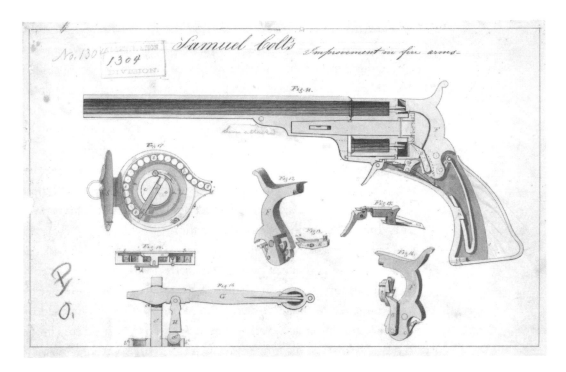

Other officers affirmed that:

a dragoon armed with Colt's repeating pistol . . . would be the most efficient and the most formidable for frontier service; and particularly when encounters with the savages occur – as they generally do – in prairies, defiles and mountain gorges. The advantages of repeating-arms in such encounters are incalculable. A few bold men, well skilled in the use of these weapons, can, under such circumstances, encounter and scatter almost any number of savages.[12]

The Great Exhibition of 1851 had been a peerless display of British engineering prowess. In particular, Joseph Whitworth, the high priest of British engineering, impressed with his stand in the hall called 'Moving Machinery' with his huge precision lathes, planing machines and measuring equipment: the new Whitworth micrometers and gauges. These

Samuel Colt's 'Improvement in fire arms' patent drawing, submitted 29 August 1839.

were the machine tools that engineered the British Empire: flexible, accurate and durable, capable of making the accurate moving parts for anything from a locomotive to a power loom. So it was a paradox that only a couple of years later British military authorities began to fret about the state of British arms manufacture and started to look towards America. In 1854 a Parliamentary Select Committee on the Manufacture of Small Arms was set up particularly to study these new 'armory' techniques. Moreover, Colt had now started a London factory near Vauxhall Bridge in Pimlico and was seen, in Britain, as the expert on the new American system. Even Charles Dickens visited his factory and admired its efficiency and organization.

The parliamentary committee, however, did not realize that Colonel Colt's system was an ingenious and less perfect variant of the u.s. government 'armory' system, so when giving evidence to the committee he was compelled to fudge. Asked if the parts of his weapons could be interchanged, he remarked airily that 'it would not cost you very much to do so.' However, his former production supervisor, Gage Stickney, went further and rather let the cat out of the bag with regard to Colt and interchangeable manufacturing, saying, 'I have heard of it, but I defy a man to show me a case.'[13] Naturally, British gunmakers were riled by the colonel's claims of perfection in manufacture. They had much to be proud of, including weapons that were highly durable and functionally almost perfect by the standard of the time. William Westley Richards, of the eminent Birmingham gunmakers Westley Richards, bought six Colt revolvers to test the claims of interchangeability for himself. Not one part was interchangeable with another, he asserted to the commission. The reason was hard for the commissioners to understand, since the philosophy and practice of mass production was novel and notions of accuracy as a relative or statistical concept, not as an ideal, were still in the process of being formulated.

America still seemed to hold the answer, however, and Joseph Whitworth went with colleagues to inspect the Springfield Armory and see the techniques at their source. They realized that while flexible, multi-purpose British machine tools could make almost anything, given time and skilled operators, America had concentrated on repetition and the high-speed production of numerous identical parts. Unlike British workshops there was a plethora of single-purpose machines refined to do one job, over and over again, and which could generally be operated by less skilled labour. The result was that American machinery was imported to re-equip the government arsenal at Enfield, while even the Birmingham gun trade was forced to consolidate to a degree, mainly to be sure of landing government contracts, forming the Birmingham Small Arms Company (BSA), which endured for many years as a powerful and expert engineering company making rifles, weapons of all kinds, motorcycles and cars until, along with so much British engineering, it ran into the sand in the 1970s.

The Winchester rifle, the Remington pistol and, above all, the Colt revolver epitomized the reliable, available and relatively cheap arms that could be purchased in hardware stores throughout the West, but, in legend at any rate, it was the Colt that triumphed. Indeed, the Colt company named one of its products, the long-barrelled Colt 45, 'The Peacemaker', helping it achieve a mythic property so strong that it attained the status of an actual character in the forthcoming genre of cowboy movies – a piece of hardware that was, in itself, as indispensable as the cast of cowboys, heroes and villains to the formal dramatic structure of the 'Western'.

Although, of course, in many Westerns, the foe is identified as in some way essentially different, these struggles with alien Indians and Mexicans in time became rather problematic tropes for American storytellers. Furthermore, long after Indian resistance was overcome by military action and the sheer tide and persistence of immigration, the American West continued as a violent world filled with dangerous and untrustworthy North Americans who could be absconders, psychopaths or adventurers from further east. There were also Civil War deserters and former veterans simply inured to violence by that war, and so the dangers in the West were not just of the conventional cinematographic kind, such as stagecoach hold-ups, bank heists or 'range wars' between the bullying cattlemen grazing the open land and the homesteaders trying to fence off a farm. It was an intensely criminalized and dangerous society. In her pioneering work *There Must be a Lone Ranger*, Jenni Calder recorded that by 1889 Oklahoma 'seethed with outcasts and refugees from the law' and was 'the scene of some of the most gruesome and irrational crime in the West'.[14]

The American foundation myth, therefore, is not just about the Lone Ranger riding to the rescue with a self-controlled and justified

The Ames gunstock-making machine – one of the many new American machines imported for the Enfield arsenal. It copies a gunstock from a 'master' pattern to replace one of the most complex of the old gunsmith's hand crafts.

use of violence. It is also about the establishment of a more wholesome society out of near chaos by will, leadership and bravery, and the idea that by resolute moral will the right kind of man – the man of principle – could actually build a new civic order. This theme is explored in numerous Westerns such as *Shane*, *High Noon* and *The Magnificent Seven*, to name just a handful of titles from a huge genre.

In his farewell statement, written shortly before his death but released posthumously on 25 August 2018, John McCain, former senator and 2008 contender for the presidency of the United States, wrote of America as 'a nation of ideals' that had helped to 'liberate more people from tyranny and poverty than ever before in history'. The way in which the shoot-out became a mythic event for film-makers connects directly to the crystallization of these ideals in the American psyche and even, it seems evident, to the formulation of American foreign policy.

One seminal event was the gunfight in Tombstone, Arizona, in 1881, when Wyatt Earp and colleagues killed three of the outlaw 'Cowboy' band. *Law and Order* (1932, dir. Edward L. Cahn) was perhaps the first film to explore the tale,[15] although much better known is *Gunfight at the OK Corral* (1957, dir. John Sturges) with Burt Lancaster as Wyatt Earp and Kirk Douglas as his buddy 'Doc' Holliday. There was also a remake of *Law and Order* (1953, dir. Nathan Juran) starring Ronald Reagan, a film apparently so awful that it has been credited with helping to end Reagan's cinematic career. Then there has been *Tombstone* (1993, dir. George P. Cosmatos) with Kurt Russell and Val Kilmer as Earp and Holliday, and *Wyatt Earp* (1994, dir. Lawrence Kasdan) with Kevin Costner. The sheer proliferation of Western films based, however loosely, on this particular event illustrates that the exploration of the painful emergence of law is fundamentally important to the genre and is, indeed, almost its *raison d'être*.

But the lawmen, it seems, could be more compromised figures than the men of principle that Hollywood chose to depict, and 'the famous sheriffs of the West were men not very different from the men they brought to justice – or briefly despatched.'[16] Even Wyatt Earp, it seems, was himself an ambiguous character who had been 'a gambler, saloon owner and pimp'.[17] Intriguingly, the new genre of 'spaghetti westerns' that emerged in the 1960s, headed by the films of Sergio Leone, come closer to reflecting this moral ambiguity than the Hollywood originals that they reflect. At the root of most of these fables is the implicit confirmation that civil society and order are precious. The mystery, for us today, in what seems like an increasingly unstable world, is how they ever became established at all.

INVENTING THE MACHINE GUN

It seems a small step from the repeating weapon, like the Colt, which is ready to fire with each trigger pull, to a fully automatic weapon that keeps on firing as long as pressure is kept on the trigger, and as long as the store of ammunition lasts. Like the power loom and the jet engine in different epochs, it seemed that the time for this invention had come and by 1860 the machine gun was ready to be devised, although it proved remarkably hard to perfect. Numerous gunsmiths and inventors were working on it. Richard Gatling's device used a rotating cluster of six or more barrels cranked round and reloaded by a handle. The multiple barrels helped reduce the tendency to overheat. Gatling (apocryphally) said he devised it to show the futility of war, to enable wars to be fought with smaller armies and to reduce the death toll. Like Samuel Colt, gun inventors seem prone to remarkably flippant remarks about their creations.

Although Gatling's weapon was invented during the American Civil War, neither army bought it due to its unreliability. However, some Union commanders bought them privately and deployed them during the siege of Petersburg, Virginia, in 1864.

There were many imitators, including William Gardner in Ohio with another hand-cranked gun that was made commercially by Pratt & Whitney, the famous engineering company that had actually been formed during the original American 'armory system' programme. The British army was convinced of the worth of the Gardner, which fired many thousands of rounds on test without fault, and shipped at least one to Egypt and the Sudan in 1884 for the expeditionary campaign to relieve General Gordon, besieged in Khartoum by the forces of the Mahdi.

But here again we meet Charles Beresford, later Admiral Lord Beresford, commanding the naval detachment that took shallow-draught paddle steamers up the Nile, each towing an assortment of the substantial open boats the navy called 'whalers' and filled with soldiers. At the shallows and rapids, men on shore had to rig tackles and cables to haul the flotilla upstream. It was a heroic undertaking for the boats had to be man-hauled over shallows and rapids: at one point, Beresford recorded that there were 1,400 men hauling on the cables.

But Gordon's situation was desperate and in January 1885 General Sir Garnet Wolseley sent part of the force overland, hoping to save time by cutting off a bight of the Nile. With them went Charles Beresford and a naval detachment with the Gardner gun. Near Abu Klea (today Abu Tuleih), about 160 km (100 mi.) from Khartoum, they met the Mahdi's mounted forces. The British forces drew up into an infantry square, an immensely strong and almost undefeatable formation that had served since the days of Waterloo. The tactical idea was that, when faced with a cavalry charge, the front rank kneeled, rifles (originally muskets) cocked, bayonets slanting upwards, but they held their fire. They were to be the last chance if a charge broke through. Behind them was a rank of soldiers at the crouch, ready to fire, and standing behind them, a third. As the charge approached, the soldiers held their fire until the enemy horsemen were only 30 or 40 yards away. Then the rear two ranks fired in volleys. The discipline and control required must have been utterly extraordinary, but maintaining it was their best chance of life. The weapons were not especially accurate and firing too soon would waste many shots. Firing too late meant horses and riders, even though fatally wounded, might plunge through the line, crushing a gap through which their fellows could leap and, once inside the square, cut up the soldiers from behind.

Beresford, with the naval brigade, had charge of the Gardner gun and ordered it dragged out of the square to the left flank. It has been suggested that he was foolhardy in placing the gun there and too keen to play with the new device. But from his own account it seems that Beresford's order to move the gun was not rash but a rational decision. He recalled that

> I saw the enemy . . . before the square was completely formed . . . thousands sprang into view on the left flank . . . They were tearing down upon us with a roar like the roar of the sea and all were chanting, as they leaped and ran, the war song of their faith . . . At this moment the left rear angle of the square was still unformed . . . the appalling danger of this open corner was instantly evident.[18]

Moreover, the rear corners of the square were always the most inherently vulnerable part:

> I ordered the crew of the Gardner gun to run it outside the square to the left flank . . . Five or six paces outside the square we dropped the trail of the gun . . . I laid the Gardner gun myself to make sure. As I fired, I saw the enemy mown down in rows, dropping like ninepins . . . after firing about forty rounds (eight turns of the lever), I lowered the elevation. I was putting in most effective work on the leading ranks . . . when the gun jammed . . . The next moment, the enemy were on top of us.[19]

Beresford received a thrust from a lance that slashed open his hand, 'but a spear was thrust right through poor Rhodes [a member of the gun crew], who was instantly killed by my side.' In fact, all of the gun crew were killed except Beresford, who, struggling to his feet, was driven back into the square by the rush of the enemy: 'I can compare the press to nothing but the crush of a theatre crowd alarmed by a cry of fire. I could draw neither sword nor pistol.'[20] Luckily his adversaries were just as handicapped and then the rear rank of the square, 'now occupying a position a few inches higher than the enemy', saw a chance to shoot past their colleagues. They fired over their heads, and in fact even between their heads, with a bullet passing through Beresford's own helmet. All the enemy who penetrated the square were cut down by this fire or by the British cavalry inside it and then, finally, 'the enemy retired . . . their desperate courage was marvellous.'[21]

The battle was too late to save General Gordon, who was killed along with the whole garrison a week or so later. When the relief force arrived, the Mahdi's flag was flying over the city.

The Gardner gun, some said, failed because of desert sand. Beresford, on the spot, says that a poorly made brass cartridge had swelled too much on firing and the extractor claw had pulled the head and rim off, leaving the rest stuck in the breech. It certainly showed that machine guns were futile unless they were utterly reliable.

After the battle the force realized that to fight through to Khartoum overland was hopeless, but the journey back to the Nile proved as tough as the battle they had just fought. The group repeatedly came under fire, improvising parapets from saddles, army biscuit boxes, dead camels and ammunition crates. The force fought and travelled for four days and three nights without sleep and with little water: 'their tongues were so swollen as to cause intense pain, their lips black, their mouths covered with white mucus.' Eventually, with the Mahdi's soldiers gathering strength ahead, and men continually falling to snipers, the square was formed again and, with its disciplined musket fire, trudged its way through to the Nile. 'The men were so exhausted that when they came up from their drink at the river they fell down like logs,' Beresford recorded.[22] He and his men then rejoined one of the paddle steamers, the *Safieh*, and fought their way back downstream with ramshackle armour and improvised gun mountings, under persistent fire from the

William Gardner demonstrating the Gardner machine gun, late 1870s.

Remington rolling block single-shot rifle. Britain had equipped the Egyptian army with these accurate American weapons, which were captured in substantial numbers by the Mahdi's forces.

shore. Now bolted down on board, the Gardner gun worked perfectly and was invaluable in helping the boats get back down the Nile. Nevertheless, they received many casualties, including a gunshot through the boiler, causing an escape of steam that scalded one stoker to death and horribly mutilated the others. It was repaired under fire with an improvised patch. Many years later Lord Kitchener found the *Safieh* abandoned and had this desperate boiler repair cut out to present to Beresford as a memento of his command of the vessel and their escape.

The land engagement at Abu Klea is thought to be the inspiration for Sir Henry Newbolt's poem 'Vitaï Lampada', famous for the repeated lines 'Play up! play up! and play the game' and written at a time when, perhaps, the Victorians were 'Romans'.[23]

> There's a breathless hush in the Close to-night
> Ten to make and the match to win –
> A bumping pitch and a blinding light,
> An hour to play and the last man in.
> And it's not for the sake of a ribboned coat,
> Or the selfish hope of a season's fame,
> But his captain's hand on his shoulder smote
> 'Play up! play up! and play the game!'
>
> The sand of the desert is sodden red,
> Red with the wreck of a square that broke;
> The Gatling's jammed and the Colonel dead,
> And the regiment blind with dust and smoke.
> The river of death has brimmed his banks,
> And England's far, and Honour a name,
> But the voice of a schoolboy rallies the ranks:
> 'Play up! play up! and play the game!'

This is the word that year by year,
While in her place the school is set,
Every one of her sons must hear,
And none that hears it dare forget.
This they all with a joyful mind
Bear through life like a torch in flame,
And falling fling to the host behind –
'Play up! play up! and play the game!'

In a telling comment on many other engagements, Beresford observed that almost half the British rifles jammed because the cartridge cases were poorly made, but the (American) Remington rifles used by the Mahdi's soldiers had solid-drawn brass cartridges that did not jam – and this in spite of some forty years of modernization of British weapons by bringing the 'American system' to the Enfield armoury. Beresford also remarked that even the British bayonets and cutlasses were shoddy and bent in the fight: 'The bayonets were blunt, because no one had thought of sharpening them. The spears of the Arabs were sharp like razors.'[24]

In spite of his hunting tattoo and his own sense of self-importance, Beresford was clearly a man of outstanding courage and had come to understand the overriding importance of quality in weapons manufacture. It was Britain's loss that, when it came to the direction of the navy, he and Jacky Fisher could not agree on this and ignore other differences.

MAXIM AND THE FLYING MACHINE GUN

These hand-cranked machine guns were generally effective, but the dream of countless inventors was to devise the fully automatic, self-acting gun. Like Samuel Colt, the repeating pistol inventor, Hiram Maxim was a bombastic, highly inventive and energetically self-promoting Yankee, a possible trigamist who told conflicting stories about his life, much of which he set out in a self-aggrandizing but extremely fascinating autobiography.[25] Growing up in Maine, he worked up near the Canadian border, inventing a clockwork automatic mousetrap for a flour mill, because the ordinary kind could catch only one mouse each. He also invented an automatic fire sprinkler, a locomotive headlight and numerous other devices. Although he had no formal training, he worked in his uncle's machine shop and as a draughtsman at a New York engineering works, and read mechanical and scientific encyclopaedias in the evening. He was also prone to fighting and, being enormously strong, sometimes simply lifted his opponent above his head to prove the futility of attacking him or, alternatively, would throw him down the steps. 'All along the frontier between Canada and the United States,' wrote Maxim, 'everyone knew who he could lick, and who could lick him.'[26]

Eventually Maxim became a specialist in gas production and gas lighting, moving from that to become an electrical engineer, claiming to have invented the incandescent electric light bulb before Edison. In 1884 he came to London to run an electric light company, but also took premises in Hatton Garden to develop a machine gun, although an eminent gunsmith advised him, 'Don't do it, thousands of men for many years have been working on guns. There are hundreds of [business] failures every year.'[27]

Most subsequent machine gun designers used a small fraction of the combustion gas, bled off from a port in the barrel, to work a piston and achieve the reloading. But Maxim opted for a different route, being familiar with rifles and their recoil from his early years in the backwoods, and devised a system in which the recoil force was used to drive the barrel back, open the breech, extract the cartridge and insert a fresh round. The whole system relied on precisely made sliding tracks, levers and springs. As Charles Beresford had found out, the ammunition also had to be equally precise and consistent, and here the Maxim gun proved to be horribly reliable.

Maxim teamed up with the Vickers Company – steel-makers and arms manufacturers – to mass produce the weapon and moved down to a mansion at Baldwyns Park, near Bexley in Kent, where he enjoyed demonstrating his gun to foreign dignitaries by using it to cut down trees on the estate. Maxim publicized his weapon relentlessly. There

A white ash tree, 46 cm (18 in.) in diameter, cut down in a few seconds with a small Maxim gun in the presence of Chinese diplomats. Maxim at right.

were other designs arriving on the market but Kaiser Wilhelm approved of the Maxim's performance in a trial against rival machine guns, declaring, 'That is the gun; there is no other', and so, surprisingly, since armies were intensely nationalistic in their choices, Britain and Germany went into the Great War with machine guns based on the same essential design.

Like Colt and like Gatling, Maxim was remarkably flippant about his device, recalling that he started work on the machine gun after a countryman remarked, 'If you want to make a pile of money, invent something that will enable these Europeans to cut each others' throats with greater facility.'[28] He also asked, with unconvincing naivety, why he was more famous for inventing a 'killing machine' than for his minor medical invention, an inhaler devised to treat bronchial infections and named by him Maxim's 'Pipe of Peace'. Meanwhile he moved on to the science of flight. He appreciated, rightly, that the science and the

Hiram Maxim, in his
words, 'showing the
gun to my grandson'.

experiments of the nineteenth century were starting to show that human flight was a serious possibility and no longer a fantasy. From 1894, in the parkland round his house, Maxim set out to create a scientific flying machine. He schemed a vast locomotive of the air, powered by two exceptionally light and powerful steam engines of his own design. The wingspan was the same as a recent Airbus 737. Maxim intended to solve the tricky and unknown issues of balance – both fore and aft, and sideways – by running the machine tethered along a specially constructed stretch of railway he had built, which would allow it to rise around 12.5 cm (5 in.) or so. It proved enormously powerful and it certainly had the capacity to lift its own weight, but the controllability was never established, for on one flight it tore itself from the restraining rail, lifting free. The steam was hastily shut off and it crashed to earth.

It is often suggested that Maxim never intended to fly it and that the machine was purely a test rig, but his own statements at the time contradict this. He wrote that after these preliminary runs to establish the balance, then 'taking one man with us to attend to the two horizontal rudders we should take our first fly, running the engine and doing the left and right steering ourselves.'[29]

There seems no doubt that what Maxim was working towards was a 'flying machine gun', since he was then a director and partner at Vickers, Sons & Maxim, whose main business, as noted, was the manufacture of armaments and who appear to have financed these fantastic experiments. Although Maxim, in an uncharacteristic moment of humility, later admitted that 'I rather over-reached myself at Baldwyn's Park,' just such a weapon did soon appear. By 1915 fighter aircraft or 'scouts' were in the air carrying two machine guns, and by 1938 the front-line British warplane had evolved to carry no fewer than eight forward-firing .303 Browning machine guns.

Maxim's flying machine at Baldwyns Park, Kent, after the crash, with Hiram Maxim at the controls.

MIKHAIL KALASHNIKOV AND THE ASSAULT RIFLE

The emergence of the assault rifle was a kind of paradox. By the end of the nineteenth century rifles were becoming far more accurate and had greater striking power. The Boer War had shown European armies the value of accurate long-range weapons and so by the First World War the British infantry standard weapon had become the famous .303 Lee-Enfield. The bullet was relatively heavy, with a hefty propellent charge contained in the familiar bottle-shaped cartridge. The sights on the Lee-Enfield rifles were adjustable from 200 to 2,000 yards, although no one, probably, expected to bring off an aimed shot at the longest range: 400 to 500 yards was the more likely distance for accurate fire. Nevertheless, the bullet still had lethal energy at 2,000 yards, and so a section of riflemen could be set to barrage fire, delivering continuous and intense volleys at long range, rather like the archers at Agincourt, and this concentrated plunging fire could certainly damage dense groups of enemy soldiers. This type of general fire was generally referred to as musketry, rather than marksmanship, and was regarded as one of the glories of the British army – or at least of the original, fully trained expeditionary force that went to France in 1914. The Lee-Enfield had a magazine containing ten rounds, and after each shot the bolt that closed the breech was opened and pulled back, ejecting the empty cartridge case. Sliding the bolt forward again picked up another fresh cartridge from the magazine below and inserted it home into the breech. The final movement, pushing the bolt lever downwards in towards the stock, locked it in place and sealed the breech. A skilled rifleman could get off fifteen aimed shots in a minute.

No doubt these rifles were the right weapons for trench warfare with lines separated by a desolate No Man's Land. But in close assaults, and when trenches were actually overrun and penetrated by opposing troops, these heavy, long and potentially accurate weapons were actually the wrong tools. What was needed was something far handier, shorter, lighter and fast-firing: a lightweight, portable machine gun. In these situations, sheer volume of fire was the critical factor. In 1918 Brigadier

General John T. Thompson in the USA anticipated the trend with his Thompson submachine gun, for he saw that the bolt-action magazine rifle was an inadequate weapon for fighting at close quarters. He initially christened his handier, quick-firing invention 'the trench broom'. The weapon later became more celebrated as the 'Chicago piano' in the hands of mobsters.

By the Second World War the emphasis was still largely on striking power, accuracy and range. It seemed counter-intuitive to military authorities to sacrifice these qualities. Maybe the answer was just to make the existing types of rifle both self-loading and capable of automatic fire. However, as it proved, the normal rifle cartridge was simply too powerful to be used in an automatic, hand-held weapon. For one thing the weapons heated up too much, making them liable to malfunction. Moreover, the recoil was simply too severe. Even a single prepared shot, with the rifle well tucked into the shoulder, gave a healthy kick. Automatic fire from a hand-held weapon that needed to be swung about was impractical and such guns would prove impossible to control. That was why machine guns had previously been heavily built and securely mounted on a tripod or carriage.

The major powers, however, did develop assault rifles using intermediate-power short cartridges that were halfway between a pistol and a rifle round. The noted designer Hugo Schmeisser's automatic weapon was, at first, disguised by German top brass as a 'machine pistol' because Hitler, recalling his own service in the First World War, thought soldiers should have a proper long rifle. Nonetheless, German soldiers were equipped with a variety of lightweight automatic weapons and it soon proved that these weapons were far more effective than the classical

The British .303 calibre Lee-Enfield was one of the world's longest serving designs, used in both the First World War and Second World War. It took its name from the government's Enfield armoury and the Scottish-American inventor James Paris Lee, who devised the reliable magazine and bolt system that gave it a high rate of fire. This example was carried by T. E. Lawrence (Lawrence of Arabia) during his campaign against Turkish forces in the Middle East.

old-style bolt-action rifle with many engagements occurring at ranges of only about 200 to 400 m (650 to 1,310 ft). The loss of accuracy in a short weapon was not that important and a degree of dispersion, or spread of bullets, was seen as an advantage, particularly when weapons were used to suppress enemy fire. Hitler, in time, also became an enthusiastic convert, christening the weapon the Sturmgewehr or assault rifle. Large numbers of the Sturmgewehr 44 were deployed for the war in Russia and it is arguably the design ancestor of all today's assault rifles.

In 1941 Mikhail Kalashnikov was a sergeant commander with a T-34 tank. Somewhere near the city of Bryansk, west of Moscow, he was wounded by shellfire in an engagement with German forces and ended up in a hospital south of Moscow. He recalled that in hospital there was frequent discussion about the merits of different weapons and the advantage that German soldiers had with their lightweight assault rifles.

Inspired, he said, by the desire to give the Soviet soldier something better, he began reading up on arms designs and sketched out a submachine gun. Leaving hospital as a convalescent, he recounted that he made his way to a railway locomotive depot where he persuaded the manager to allow him to use the workshop. Some months later a functional automatic weapon resulted. According to the various histories of these times that have come down to us, this original weapon was not to be the prototype of the Kalashnikov itself, but it showed his ability and commitment. One way or another he eventually found his way to the Dzerzhinsky Ordnance Academy and was encouraged to study arms design formally.

During and after the Second World War various Soviet design groups worked competitively on a new assault rifle, but Kalashnikov's design apparently triumphed. In what may be an apocryphal event, but as related by Kalashnikov himself, towards the end of this competition he met the eminent arms designer General Vasily Degtyarev, who proclaimed that 'the way Sergeant Kalashnikov has put the components of his model together is much more ingenious than mine. His model has more of a future – of that I'm certain. I no longer wish to participate in the final phase of the competition.'[30]

General Thompson with his invention – the 'trench sweeper' or trench broom'. It was developed in Cleveland, Ohio, and was ready for shipment in 1918, too late for the First World War.

Some have speculated that Kalashnikov borrowed features from the other design groups, claiming that he was more a 'magpie inventor' than a true innovator, seizing ideas from many different sources. But what designer does not, whether consciously or unconsciously? Some even speculate that Kalashnikov, as a wounded combatant from the Great Patriotic War, was merely a convenient Soviet figurehead for a larger anonymous design team. Others like to believe that Hugo Schmeisser played a part since, following the German collapse, he worked on weapons development in the Soviet Union until 1952.

There is no way to resolve these questions and Kalashnikov always vigorously rebutted them. There seems no doubt that Kalashnikov was an ingenious, creative and mechanically adept designer. And, after all, we readily accept that Frank Whittle, a Royal Air Force pilot officer, initially with little formal engineering training, invented an engine that revolutionized aviation. Is it any more surprising that a self-taught tank sergeant should devise a successful assault rifle?

The Kalashnikov rifle showed that simplicity can be best. It is not the lightest in its class, nor the most accurate, but it is commended particularly for being 'soldier-proof' even in comparatively untrained hands. A particular feature that was to contribute to its reputation for resilience was that the fits between its working components are intentionally loose, with the exception of the bolt, which must accurately seal the breach. These generous clearances give it exceptional resistance to gas fouling, dust, sand and moisture.

STONER AND THE ARMALITE

The American counterpart to the Kalashnikov was the MI6 carbine and it arose from a quite different national culture. The primary objective was again to put more firepower in the hands of the individual infantryman but unlike the Kalashnikov, which used tough and tested techniques and traditional components to make an incredibly robust weapon, the MI6 grew out of the highly technocratic American aerospace community. The design clearly reflected the different outlooks and goals in the USA and the USSR. It would be a close-range automatic-fire weapon like the Kalashnikov, but it would not compromise so much on accuracy. And it would be lighter. But like the Kalashnikov, the American rifle eventually realized as the M16 had its own curious history and its own cast of personalities.

The first step on the road to the M16 was the formation of the ArmaLite company. The name said it, for ArmaLite would use aerospace techniques to save weight and turned its back on many traditional gunsmithing practices. The 'furniture' (the wooden stock and grips) would now be made from high-tech plastics. The main body of the weapon or 'receiver' (usually called the 'action' or action body in British usage) would not be milled from steel but from high-grade aluminium aircraft alloy, and similarly the barrel might be aluminium with just a thin steel liner.

ArmaLite was the particular brainchild of George Sullivan, an engineer and patent attorney to the Lockheed aircraft company. Among his contacts was Richard Boutelle, head of the Fairchild aviation company and also a gun buff, who financed ArmaLite as an offshoot of Fairchild. One day Sullivan met Eugene Stoner, who was trying out a gun of his own design at a firing range. Stoner had formerly been an armorer with the U.S. Marines in the Second World War, servicing and repairing all types of weapons. In time he became a talented self-taught weapons designer and was now an aviation design engineer. The two hit it off and soon Stoner was installed at ArmaLite as chief designer.

The original ArmaLite was light, versatile and uncompromisingly hi-tech. And since the whole point of the assault rifle was to deliver awesome firepower, Stoner designed it to fire a tiny round (a bullet and cartridge) only .223 inches in diameter, hardly larger than the calibre of a farmer's vermin rifle. Stoner's reasoning was that he could design the weapon to give a terrific rate of fire, but that would be pointless if soldiers ran out of ammunition. For the infantryman, weight of equipment is everything and with the small and light rounds fired by the ArmaLite the infantryman could carry nearly twice as much ammunition compared to the older 'full power' American M14 rifle with its hefty .308-inch round.[31]

Stoner, however, was not prepared to sacrifice striking power, and so the ArmaLite had a powerful cartridge, giving it a muzzle velocity about 50 per cent greater than the Kalashnikov. This meant that, in terms of lethality, or striking energy, the ArmaLite and the Kalashnikov were comparable, although its high muzzle velocity meant that the M16 had a flatter trajectory (less bullet drop) and was more accurate at longer ranges.

The ArmaLite company, however, did not really prosper or land enough contracts to make it secure. Eventually it sold its principal designs out to Colt. In the meantime, though, it did appeal to General Curtis LeMay, head of the U.S. Air Force (and famous, among other things, for his threat to bomb North Vietnam 'into the Stone Age'). According to legend, Richard Boutelle invited LeMay to a birthday cook out at his ranch, where three watermelons were set up at 50, 100 and 150 yards. LeMay was handed the AR-15 rifle to try and picked off the watermelon at 50 yards and then one at 150 yards.

What impressed LeMay deeply was that the big fruits had literally blown apart. The AR-15 bullet was tiny, long, and travelled at very high velocity. The dynamics of this combination meant that when it hit the target it did not travel on cleanly through. Instead it tumbled, delivering all its energy in a local, explosive way. The watermelon demonstration argued for the weapon's enormous wounding potential, or in the politer language of small arms, 'stopping power'. Asked if he wanted to shoot the third watermelon, LeMay, by now convinced, replied, 'Hell, no – let's eat it.'[32]

LeMay's order of 80,000 rifles for the Air Force was a start, but did not guarantee the adoption of the rifle as a general infantry arm. However, by 1962 the U.S. Army badly needed to update its standard infantry weapon, for this was the time when American involvement in Vietnam was beginning to hot up, and the engagements there showed that the Soviet Union had stolen a march on the USA with the Kalashnikov, especially in the close-combat conditions of jungle warfare. America needed to upgrade its standard infantry rifle.

Secretary of Defense Robert S. McNamara had been one of the celebrated band of 'whizz kids': Second World War planners who had been trained in scientific management and in statistical control. In the post-war era many of them became eminent in national affairs, and especially in the Ford Motor Company where McNamara became company president before being recruited by John F. Kennedy for government service.

In what was, in effect, a foretaste of the anti-statist policies of Keith Joseph and Margaret Thatcher, McNamara considered that America's state-run armouries did not offer value. These venerable armouries had ushered in a revolution in arms production, and in manufacturing, but now seemed to him to be an anachronism. Why couldn't private industry offer a better, cheaper and more responsive service? One of McNamara's first, revolutionary, actions was to close the Springfield Armory, one of the birthplaces of the American system of arms manufacture and then almost two hundred years old. He also began to roll up the other armouries and weapons establishments into one procurement agency.

In Vietnam, while the army discovered that its traditional rifle no longer suited the war it was engaged in, the state armouries were contracting. At the same time the Colt company happened to have acquired the rights to the revolutionary, lightweight ArmaLite designs. The stage was set and the ArmaLite AR-15, or the M16 as it was now named for the army, seemed like the obvious solution.

But somehow, between the now compressed government arms procurement system and Colt's contract to bring in the new weapon at speed, the development process stumbled. In what turned out to be a rushed and poorly managed programme, the M16s, as first delivered in Vietnam, proved to be greatly inferior to the performance promised by the earlier ArmaLites. Curiously, as Colt and the design team, which included the originator, Eugene Stoner, brought the weapon to readiness, a separate and unconnected department in army procurement changed the cartridge and the kind of propellant (powder) it contained. This meant that the ammunition supplied for the weapons in Vietnam was not the same as that which had been used during the weapon's development.

Automatic weapons and their ammunition are closely linked. The new powder gave about 25 per cent more pressure, which some may have thought was a good thing, but it caused the M16s to fire at the much higher rate of 1,000 rounds a minute (instead of 700–800) and increased the loads on the mechanism. Moreover, the new powder was 'dirtier'. It generated more residue and in a gas-powered automatic weapon some of this residue inevitably is deposited inside the mechanism, helping to foul it. Moreover, the chosen materials of the rifle were wrong. In combination with the powder residue, the humidity and heat of Vietnam caused critical internal components to corrode, in fact to begin to rust. But perhaps the overriding problem was the increased gas pressure of the new cartridge. On firing, it would expand the cartridge case more violently in the breach, tending to anchor it there.

A split second after an automatic weapon fires, the extractor (a kind of claw mechanism) starts to pull the spent cartridge out of the breech but, as James L. Sullivan, a designer who worked with Stoner on the original ArmaLite AR-15 observed drily, 'the extractor would start to pull [the cartridge] out and then pop loose occasionally. In a weapon you can't have occasionally.'[33]

The jams of the M16 became a national scandal. In Vietnam, assault units were overrun and men died. Soldiers in combat scrambled to grab weapons from dead or wounded comrades, to find that they too would jam, until they ran out of functioning rifles to fire. They had suffered from the same problem that occurred with Lord Beresford's Gardner gun, when his crew was overrun in the Sudan nearly two hundred years before. As Beresford had also noted, matching the weapon with its ammunition was crucial.

In Vietnam some officers risked their careers to go public with their criticism. Regular servicemen wrote home privately to their parents about their problems with the weapons and worried parents wrote to their congressmen. On top of the cartridge problem, and the corrosion problem, it transpired that many units had no cleaning kits or cleaning rods. The problems with the rifle became a public scandal and a congressional committee was formed to investigate. Colt and the government agencies finally pulled together to correct the faults and the M16 eventually achieved everything that was originally promised for it.

Private Michael J. Mendoza uses his M16 rifle to recon by fire during the Vietnam War, 8 September 1967.

But how did it all go so wrong? The repeating firearm was, by then, an old and well-understood invention, but nevertheless it is an extraordinarily intricate and sensitive mechanism and every design change brings new challenges. The materials, the form, the hardness, the tensile strength and the chemistry of every part must be selected, refined and trialled with extraordinary care.

The old armouries were thorough, slow maybe, and perhaps expensive, but they saw it as a sacred duty to put functionally perfect weapons in the hands of soldiers. But beyond the processes to design and develop the weapons is the complex logistical system that delivers them to fighting units together with the right ammunition, the cleaning kits and the right oil.

Perhaps because of McNamara's reforms at a time of pressure and the rush to get the new arms into the field, this human machine simply stumbled. Compared to the Kalashnikov programme, the American M16 programme was a train crash between old-style, but fading, state armoury control and American industrial practice. One author has written that, at this time 'the American system was neither capitalist nor fully state-driven. It was a disharmonious hybrid.'[34]

CONCLUSION

Kalashnikov spent his later years 'like Chekhov's wedding general', wheeled out like a distinguished senior relative on ceremonial occasions or to help Russian trade missions.[35] He travelled widely and in America even met Eugene Stoner, his great rival in assault rifle design. The two got on famously, discussing their careers and their lives as weapons designers. The odd thing, noted one observer, was that, though the two had never met before, 'they appeared to know each other well.'[36] The photograph of the meeting is one of the many mind-shifting and bizarre records from the world of arms. Here are two men in late middle age, smartly dressed in jackets and ties, smiling, genial – they could be senior uncles meeting at a family reunion – except that each is indissolubly associated with an assault rifle of almost unrivalled lethality. And as a gesture of gentle courtesy, each is holding an example of the other man's design.

Though feted as a hero of the Soviet era, Kalashnikov clearly felt that he had not reaped the right material rewards, even in the new, post-Communist Russia. He lived modestly and grumbled that 'Stoner has his own aeroplane,' although in terms of profusion Kalashnikov was clearly the winner with something like 100 million examples of his weapon in existence.[37] Second place, a mere 10 million, is held by Stoner's designs.

The reason for the disparity, of course, was that the Kalashnikov was, above all, a product of the Cold War. At its height, the USSR and the Warsaw Pact countries had the largest integrated land army the world had ever seen, with millions of men under arms, and it used the AK-47 as a standardized assault rifle, whether they were front-line troops, cooks or airfield guards. This in itself led to a huge output from the original factory in Izhevsk (an armoury town even in Tsarist times). The numbers used by the USSR and its immediate satellites were compounded by large-scale exports around the world as aid to sympathetic states and to revolutionary groups fighting internal wars. They were also manufactured under licence in an extraordinary number of countries, including Albania, China, East Germany and Poland – and so the Kalashnikov became the most abundant weapon on earth. In many parts of the world the market price of Kalashnikovs has become a kind of stock market index of insecurity.

Kalashnikov himself was as insouciant about his gun invention as were Gatling and Colt, regarding its creation as a patriotic act and saying, at the sixtieth anniversary of the gun in 2007, that 'I sleep well. It's the politicians who are to blame for failing to come to an agreement and resorting to violence.'[38]

The idea that a kind of Darwinian evolution operates for machines and inventions used to be a conventional model in the history of technology. Subsequent history resisted this kind of technological determinism, for there were always intriguing alternatives, the roads not taken, or ones tentatively tried: the v2 rocket instead of the Lancaster bomber; Brunel's broad-gauge railway against Stephenson's narrow; the monorail and 'dude, where's my flying car'? But even if many technological

Mikhail Kalashnikov (right) with Eugene Stoner, designer of the ArmaLite and the M16, in 1990. Each is holding the rifle designed by the other.

A child soldier in
Monrovia, Liberia,
with an AK-47, 2003.

choices can only be explained by their socio-political context, the route
from the repeating weapons like the Colt, through heavy machine guns
of increasing firepower, to the light, portable, automatic assault rifle
seems remarkably linear. Even if social conditions and human agency
presented various choices, they seemed to only have had one result.
From the nineteenth-century American 'armory project', to the Colt,
the Maxim and the Kalashnikov, the tale is the remorseless spread of
arms and the multiplication of the firepower and lethality that can be
wielded by an individual.[39]

Today assault rifles are commonplace in private hands in many
countries, but probably no country has as many, or as many per head,
as the USA where, for complex historical and legal reasons, there are no
official government statistics on ownership, although it is estimated that
between 8 million and 15 million of these assault weapons have been
sold. Moves towards gun control, however tentative, seem to encourage

sales and so do mass shootings, which give gun owners concern that new restrictions may result.

Surprisingly, many Americans own Kalashnikovs, impressed by its sturdy functionalism, although it is Stoner's M16 that is cherished as 'America's rifle' by gun buffs, who regard its creator as a popular hero. In contrast to the many curious and self-serving things said by firearms inventors, Stoner was retiring and modest. According to legend, Kalashnikov joshed him at one of their meetings with the assertion by boastfully claiming that his own rifle had won revolutions, had fought tyranny and was the most reliable in the world. Stoner replied, 'I just get a royalty check every month.'[40]

7

FROM DEATH RAYS
TO STAR WARS

And then . . . I noted a little black knot of men, the foremost of whom was waving a white flag . . . Suddenly there was a flash of light, and a quantity of luminous greenish smoke came out of the pit in three distinct puffs . . . Forthwith flashes of actual flame, a bright glare leaping from one to another, sprang from the scattered group of men. It was as if some invisible jet impinged upon them and flashed into white flame. It was as if each man were suddenly and momentarily turned to fire.

Then, by the light of their own destruction, I saw them stagger-ing and falling, and their supporters turning to run.

I stood staring, not as yet realising that this was death leaping from man to man in that little distant crowd . . . An almost noise-less and blinding flash of light, and a man fell headlong and lay still; and as the unseen shaft of heat passed over them, pine-trees burst into fire . . . It was sweeping round swiftly and steadily, this flaming death, this invisible, inevitable sword of heat.[1]

This, of course, is H. G. Wells's account of the Martian heat ray in *The War of the Worlds* (1898). With its 'thread of green fire', Wells's invention seems like an extraordinarily prescient account of the beam or laser weapons that are, only now, beginning to appear feasible.

Although it is claimed that the exotic Serbian electrical inventor Nikola Tesla devised a high-frequency electrical beam energy weapon in the 1930s (and was rumoured to have offered it to the British government for $30 million), in the real world the 'death ray' was considered quite fantastical. It became a staple of pulp science-fiction comics and prototypical space heroes like Flash Gordon.

Nevertheless, in 1934 H. E. Wimperis, Director of Scientific Research at the Air Ministry, was bold enough to ask if it might now be possible to deliver enough energy in the form of radio waves to stop the engine of a hostile aircraft, or to disable its human crew. With increasing apprehension about the scale of German rearmament, and with feverish rumours of a Nazi death-ray in the air, Wimperis mused that 'in view of the urgency no avenue however seemingly fantastic must be left unexplored' and 'one of the coming things will be the transmission by radiation of large amounts of electric energy'; he therefore sought advice from the physiologist and anti-aircraft gunnery pioneer A. V. Hill.[2] Could a debilitating amount of energy be projected by radio waves? He learned from Hill that 'in a laboratory experiment on these lines the skin was burnt off the tail of a rat,' and so a cagey enquiry was then passed to Robert Watson-Watt of the government's Radio Research Station. He was careful to disguise his intentions and merely asked Watson-Watt to make some calculations as to whether radio waves could possibly raise the temperature of a certain quantity of water by two degrees centigrade at a distance. Watson-Watt, though, was not deceived, realizing that this was the amount of water in a human body. He recalled sardonically that he 'saw at once that what was wanted was the low-brow death ray'. This episode, famously, marked the birth of British radar.[3]

THE LASER'S FINEST HOUR

The invention of the laser in the late 1950s triggered a revival of the notion of a beam weapon. Lasers were feeble things at first, but their ability to generate a tight, high-power beam that did not spread or dissipate over distance was then quite new and seemed almost magical. It even appeared to suggest that a beam weapon was possible. By the late 1970s research had pushed up the power enough for lasers to become widely used in industry for cutting various materials, including sheet metal.

Meanwhile, the physicist George Chapline, working at the Lawrence Livermore National Laboratory, had been following Soviet academic work on X-ray lasers. X-rays have a far shorter wavelength than visible light, which means that they can have far more destructive energy, and so this research inevitably led to the suspicion that the Soviet Union was extending the work in secret to develop a weapon.

Chapline's innovation was to propose driving the laser with a small nuclear explosion. The concept was that a bundle of metal rods would be energized or 'pumped' by the X-rays emitted by the detonation. The rods, of course, would be vapourised in a trice, but before that, it was believed, they would emit a powerful burst of X-rays, amplified and aimed in a coherent beam by these lasing rods. Chapline and colleagues set out to prove the concept with a number of underground nuclear test explosions.

From the outset it was seen that the X-ray laser, if it could be made to work, would be a candidate for anti-ballistic missile defence and the idea was to find support in a surprising quarter. In 1976 the Princeton physicist Gerard K. O'Neill published his book *The High Frontier: Human Colonies in Space*, a work that became the manifesto of the emerging, countercultural space advocacy groups like the L5 Society – so named after the Lagrange points, positions of gravitational equilibrium in the solar system and therefore thought to be good sites for future space colonies.

The L5 movement was an intriguing Utopian movement that saw the Apollo Moon landings as merely the prelude to a much more ambitious programme of O'Neill-type colonies. It was influenced by the 1972 MIT report *The Limits to Growth*, which had been commissioned by the Club of Rome, an international think tank composed of senior politicians, scientists and economists who saw overpopulation and the depletion of resources and energy as a major threat to civilization.[4]

The founders of the L5 Society, Carolyn and Keith Henson, argued that space colonization was needed to escape this looming crisis. By 1976 they had added nuclear war to the list of imminent risks and reluctantly began to push for space defences. Part of their space settlement scheme included huge solar arrays in space, which could beam power back to

Earth, and so it seemed attractive to also use this power source to drive the new, promised laser weapons. Perhaps the Hensons also concluded that only a military space programme could unlock the enormous funds and recruit the massive industrial and economic effort that would be required to create what was their real objective: large, peopled space settlements.

THE HIGH FRONTIER GROUP

When the Star Wars programme emerged in America in the 1980s many regarded it as a fantastic dream from the most extreme techno-boosters in the defence community, but it had arisen out of an increasing conundrum about the basing policies (the launch site locations) for the u.s. missile force. To the u.s. strategists it seemed that the Soviet preponderance in pure numbers of land-based intercontinental ballistic missiles (ICBMs), as well as their greater 'throw weight' compared to u.s. weapons, was creating a new kind of strategic uncertainty. Moreover, increasing numbers were equipped with multiple, independently steerable warheads (MIRVs). No doubt the situation looked different to Soviet analysts, who were well aware of other u.s. nuclear assets such as air-launched bombs and stand-off missiles from the B-52 aircraft fleet, as well as the growing submarine missile fleet. In America, however, the huge Soviet land-based missile capability seemed to undermine the principle of 'mutually assured destruction' on which the edgy stability of the Cold War depended.

In this new scenario, it was feared that the Soviets might be able to destroy the American retaliatory force with a surprise first strike, while still retaining a large proportion of their missile force in reserve to compel complete surrender.

This apparent insecurity of the land-based ICBMs pushed u.s. defence planners to consider increasingly exotic solutions, for example a fleet of MX missiles stationed around a vast 'racetrack' or railway in Nevada or North and South Dakota, with a large number of launch bases (silos) around it. At any time, many silos would be empty and the missiles would be moved by night from one to another to defeat Soviet targeting plans.

Any basing solution, however, might conceal a dangerous trap – 'a strategic valley of death' – like the penultimate move in a chess game that could suddenly expose a fatal checkmate. Perhaps the USA might commit to new defensive arrangements and locations for missile sites only to find that the whole effort was nullified by some new spasm of Soviet missile construction or invention. The USA, they felt, no longer had the industrial base to outproduce the Soviet Union in sheer numbers of weapons, but its unquestioned lead in technology might produce a new strategic edge.

Out of this frustration emerged an odd, non-governmental body that probably could not have existed anywhere except in the USA. It was launched by Daniel Graham, a retired general, former director of the Defense Intelligence Agency and a presidential campaign adviser for Ronald Reagan. He teamed up with Karl R. Bendetsen, a high-level civil servant and former Under Secretary of the Army, to form a new independent body called High Frontier Inc., which sought funds from private foundations and wealthy individuals like the brewing magnate Joseph Coors, who was a friend of Ronald Reagan's and a contributor to his presidential campaign. The group was often at odds with formal government defence thinking in the Pentagon and it should, perhaps, be thought of as part pressure group, part think tank, and with loose, personal, more or less informal links to the administration and to the military. The name High Frontier, of course, reflected the fears of the founder that the Soviets were seeking military dominance in space and that this would nullify the U.S. deterrent force. Space was the new high frontier and one aim was to make Reagan adopt space-based missile defences as U.S. policy.

To Graham and his associates a huge national effort along the lines of the Manhattan Project, which delivered the atomic bomb in the Second World War, would deliver such a demanding suite of new technologies: specially managed arrangements that would remove the project from regular governmental channels. As a major plank in their scheme they also adopted the L5 Society's idea of large space settlements with solar power collectors, which now would power the hoped-for laser weapons.

The scheme was outlined in March 1982 with the publication of *High Frontier: A New National Strategy*. The project would have unofficial status outside the government and a projected cost intially estimated at between $10 billion and $40 billion by Graham's group. However, these figures were continually revised upwards and by 1984 were being reckoned by some analysts as likely to reach between $400 billion and $800 billion. However, Boeing, it was claimed, considered that the system could destroy 95 per cent of incoming missiles.

EDWARD TELLER

Meanwhile, the defence scientist and physicist Edward Teller continually promoted the X-ray laser. Teller was enthusiastic about all possible ideas for ballistic missile defence, but particularly about the nuclear-pumped X-ray laser, which eventually was named Excalibur. As former laboratory director at the Lawrence Livermore facility (established at the height of the Cold War to develop new nuclear weapons), and subsequently associate director there, he was well aware of all developments in the laser and could also influence the research programme, which he talked up shamelessly, perhaps on the basis that 'you can't lie about the future' and that if enough funds were forthcoming, the physics would follow and research would make it a reality.

Throughout this period Teller campaigned vigorously. An associate recalled that, as he spoke about X-ray defence, 'he seemed to shake with excitement' and his vibrations recalled a student engineering problem: 'the reed vibrates most vigorously at its natural resonant frequency.' During this period Teller declared that 'he was in the same state of frustration that he had experienced earlier when trying to convince u.s. leaders that it was necessary to develop the hydrogen bomb.'[5]

Teller finally got a chance to argue for the space defence scheme to President Ronald Reagan in July 1982. Interviewed by Bill Buckley on his PBS television show, Teller mused that 'from the time that President Reagan has been nominated, I have not had a single opportunity to talk to him . . . I am deeply grateful for any opportunity to talk about [strategic defence].'⁶

Reagan, it seems, saw that broadcast and a series of meetings followed that appeared to be less decisive than Teller hoped, although Reagan steadily moved towards the policy of developing a new anti-missile system. It is not clear, however, whether it was Teller's advocacy that was crucial, or whether the High Frontier group was equally respon-sible. What is known is that Reagan was deeply unhappy with the notion of mutually assured destruction and had a gut feeling that there ought to be a way of removing the existential threat of nuclear weapons. Simultaneously with the lobbying and the X-ray research, Reagan was

Artist's impression of the Excalibur X-ray laser destroying incoming nuclear missiles, c. 1983.

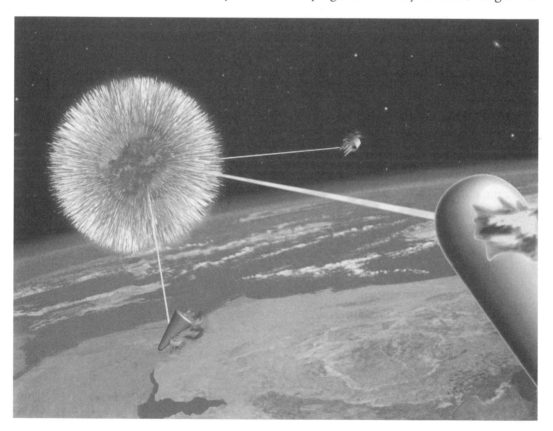

musing: 'what if we began to move away from our total reliance on offense to deter a nuclear attack and moved towards a relatively greater reliance on defense?'

The efforts of Edward Teller and of the High Frontier group culminated in the televised speech to the nation that President Ronald Reagan made on 23 March 1983, announcing the start of a massive research programme on a defence against nuclear missiles. He reflected on the necessity of relying on mutual destruction, 'the specter of retaliation, on mutual threat', for current security:

> and that's a sad commentary on the human condition. Wouldn't it be better to save lives than to avenge them? Are we not capable of demonstrating our peaceful intentions by applying all our abilities and our ingenuity to achieving a truly lasting stability? . . . Indeed, we must . . . Let me share with you a vision of the future that offers hope.[7]

The speech marked the start, in the public domain, of what became known as the Strategic Defense Initiative (SDI), although from its critics it soon acquired the derisive title of 'Star Wars'. Cold War historian John Lewis Gaddis has made the point convincingly that Ronald Reagan was deeply committed to it and its possibilities. But there was inevitably a spectrum of views on it, and many policy advisers perhaps did not have high expectations of SDI, although they expected that if defence techno-science received an awful lot of money then something useful might emerge, that a defence might be possible and that American technology might finally deliver one.[8]

In spite of his real, and perhaps naive, hopes for SDI, Reagan was wily enough to see that the programme was also a useful diplomatic instrument. In 1982 he made this thought more explicit with a remark at a National Security Council meeting: 'Why don't we just lean on the Soviets until they go broke?' He showed that this was not simply a rhetorical remark by adding, 'that's the direction we are going to go.' Reagan followed up these remarks with formal, secret commitments in

President Ronald Reagan addressing the nation: his 'Star Wars' television speech on 23 March 1983.

National Security Decision Directives. Richard E. Pipes has described one of these, NSDD-75, as 'the first document that said that what mattered was not only Soviet behavior but the nature of the Soviet system. NSDD-75 said our goal was no longer to coexist with the Soviet Union but to change the Soviet system.'[9]

And so, whatever the possibilities of Star Wars, some supported it for subtler political and strategic motives and for the additional appeal that it would force U.S.–Soviet competition into the highest reaches of technology, where they believed America would always have the advantage.

What most accounts of the 'Star Wars' episode omit is that one of the principal attractions of the new technology was that it was so expensive, for some U.S. policymakers had come to believe that the USSR was a sick society, struggling under the burden of its vast military machine and delivering an increasingly impoverished lifestyle to its subjects. One senator even conducted his own demographic research with aides combing the death notice columns of Soviet newspapers to prove that life expectancy and health were declining. Could an escalation of the cost and technical complexity of defence break the camel's back?

At the conference 'The Cold War and its Legacy', hosted by Churchill College, Cambridge, in 2009, a former White House policy adviser gave an account of a defence discussion that Reagan held with his staff and military advisers, and there must have been many like it. They tallied the numbers of ballistic missiles the U.S. held compared to the Soviet Union. It had more aircraft, more land-based missile delivery systems, more tanks and so on. The disparity was depressing. With each report the president said nothing. Submarines, tanks and infantry – the dismal toll went on and on. In sheer numbers, the U.S. was inferior in every department, and though many believed in a qualitative superiority of U.S. weaponry, no one knew what advantage that might amount to in a real war. Eventually Reagan turned to his old friend Bill Casey, the new CIA director, and asked, 'What have we got more of than the Soviets?' 'Money,' he answered, 'we've got more money.' 'Well' replied Reagan, 'we'll use the money.'[10]

Later someone asked if that meant it had not mattered whether Star Wars had worked or not. 'It was a *device*,' the White House adviser replied meaningfully. And then, just in case there was any ambiguity about what sort of device he meant, he added, 'there was always someone you could wheel out to explain why it had to cost so much.'

Not everyone, however, agrees that SDI was merely a diplomatic instrument. Cold War historian John Lewis Gaddis paints Reagan as a sincere nuclear abolitionist trying to negotiate 'real and verifiable reductions in the world's nuclear arsenals and one day, with God's help, their total elimination'. Reagan, he argues, was genuinely committed to SDI and hoped it would work. Nevertheless, it was still a useful tool to add pressure in negotiations. Both thoughts were evident in a comment Reagan made in discussion: 'Wouldn't it be better to protect the American people than avenge them? . . . Don't lose those words.'[11]

President Reagan and Edward Teller at the White House in January 1989.

Unfortunately for the advocates of SDI, the programme arrived at a time when anti-war activism among American academics had grown in response to the Vietnam War. Many college campuses became explicitly anti-militarist and scientists began to resist the influence of defence funding on research. Hostility to Star Wars spread across almost the entire academic scientific community. As a noted hawk, and as 'father of the H-bomb', Edward Teller's advocacy of SDI and of the bomb-driven X-ray laser certainly also helped polarize the academic scientific community against it.

Even MIT, which had played a leading part in defence research for decades, turned against SDI. This was surprising because in the Second World War it had made striking contributions to military radar through the famous 'Rad Lab', and in the post-war era had been crucial to the development of ballistic missile navigation systems, becoming the biggest non-industrial military contractor (see Chapter Five). MIT labs had also played an active part during the Vietnam War, including the development of esoteric 'people detectors' for monitoring Viet Cong tunnels and remote jungle trails.

Opposition to these military links grew throughout that period and in 1969 the Union of Concerned Scientists was formed by both staff and students there with the aim of devising 'means for turning research applications away from the present emphasis on military technology toward the solution of pressing environmental and social problems'.[12]

By 1985 the mood had hardened so far that MIT president Paul Gray, in a graduation day speech, condemned the Pentagon's research contracts on SDI systems as a 'manipulative effort' to win 'implicit institutional endorsement for SDI', and concluded that 'this university will not be so used.'[13] To academic opponents of Star Wars, the scheme was technically unfeasible but, paradoxically, also politically unwise, dangerous and destabilizing. Gradually the SDI programme wound down. It had spent some $26 billion over ten years and launched a dozen spacecraft. The data on the nuclear pumped laser had been equivocal. The technical difficulty of creating and launching enough space battle stations seemed intimidating. Moreover, the whole scheme was open to the objection that it could be countered by the Soviets simply building more missiles or decoys for much less than the SDI umbrella would cost the USA.[14]

AFTER STAR WARS

Lasers are widely used today as sighting aids for firearms and munitions. A laser mounted on a conventional weapon can throw a spot of light to show the gun crew or a soldier where the shot will strike. They are also used as target designators, with the laser being used to paint a target, while a smart bomb or missile homes on its particular wavelength. However, it has proved hard to develop the laser to deliver a truly disruptive amount of energy. Nevertheless, the American warship USS *Ponce* was fitted with an experimental laser weapon of some 30 kWh, which was said to be effective against lighter targets such as drones, light aircraft, helicopters and motorboats. A ship can carry a substantial payload, but for land use the large size of the electrical power supply that is needed means that so far the weapons are moveable but not mobile. Experimental models, however, have been tested successfully against mortar rounds in flight, drones and some missiles.

Laser power keeps creeping up and chemical combustion lasers have been devised: in effect, jet engines that burn fuel and produce an intense lasing or light-emitting combustion zone. One roadblock is that at high energies the laser beam causes the intervening air molecules to 'bloom' or split apart into plasma (positive and negative particles), becoming opaque, defocusing the beam and dispersing its energy into the atmosphere. But human ingenuity being what it is, researchers have realized that this plasma is far more electrically conductive than air, and so it might be possible with an 'electrolaser' to send a jolt of high-energy electricity down this transient new plasma pathway. This would, in effect, be a man-made version of Zeus' lightning bolt, but so far as we know no one has yet made it work. A variant of the laser, said to be under development by the U.S. military, is a 'pulsed energy projectile', a burst of infrared energy that instantly vaporizes a small amount of the target surface. This smoke is then instantly cooked up by another ensuing laser pulse, causing an explosive shockwave that knocks a person off their feet.

Another possibility has been the Neutral Particle Beam (NPB) weapon, which is a hypothetical development of laboratory atomic accelerators. Accelerators are massive fixed installations that accelerate hydrogen atoms with millions of volts through a long accelerating tunnel, with powerful magnets to steer the beam. This was also tipped, like the laser, as a possible technology for anti-ballistic missile defence, in spite of the almost unimaginable challenge to create a deployable weapon consisting of a long accelerator tunnel with all its ancillaries, magnets, controls and the massive electricity-generating capacity to drive it.

All these possible next-generation weapons, whether based on beams or on speculative devices firing high-energy electrically-propelled projectiles (rail guns), demonstrate one tremendous advantage that old-style weapons still have: the enormous energy density of their ammunition. Bullets and shells are driven by chemicals – propellants – that are really just tamed versions of high explosives and their special property is that they contain an immense amount of energy for their size, but can also release it in a fraction of a second. The cartridge that sends a rifle bullet several miles is slightly smaller than a lipstick. The

Experimental laser weapon on the battleship USS *Ponce* while deployed to the Arabian Gulf, 2014.

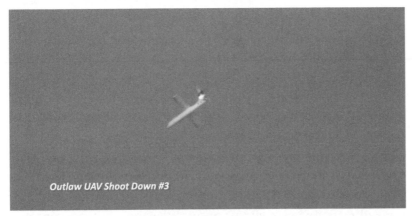

Outlaw UAV Shoot Down #3

Drone aircraft struck by an experimental Lockheed-Martin laser weapon prior to crash. The heat beam buckles and destroys the tail structure. Critics say that the weapon is only effective against thin-skinned targets, like motorboats or lightweight drones, and that 'like a mirage, the laser weapon is always just over the horizon'.

charges that fire field guns are around the size of a couple of loaves of bread. To get an electrical battery to store electrical power in similarly compact packages, and to release it in a similar timescale to conventional propellants, has so far proved impossible. If achieved, it would also mean that these batteries were, potentially, explosive packages in their own right, and clearly dangerous if subject to some mishap.

And so no one, it seems, has yet come up with a feasible scheme for practical battlefield beam weapons, though they do seem inevitably to be creeping closer. A slightly different kind of weapon does exist. U.S.-based Raytheon's 'Active Denial System', called by some the 'pain beam', is a focused beam of radio energy, much like that in a microwave oven, intended to provide a non-lethal riot control or area denial weapon. It generates an intense feeling of heat and an urgent compulsion to run away and some describe it as being like a hot oven or grill being opened up. This may well be deployed, for authorities know that tear gas is inefficient and unpredictable and water cannons are short in range. Authorities generally wish to avoid killing significant numbers of dissidents, partly out of humanitarian instinct, but also because of international reputational damage. It is this that gives unarmed and courageous protest its moral force, as Gandhi knew. Powerful long-range and largely non-lethal weapons in the hands of illiberal regimes may be a new step in human affairs since peaceful, unarmed protests or gatherings could easily be dispersed.

The beam weapon is essentially a mythic weapon, the ultimately idealized gun with an unerringly straight and flat trajectory, reaching out at the speed of light. It seems almost inevitable that lethal beam weapons of some kind will be deployed in time. Although H. G. Wells envisaged the death ray in 1898 and Ronald Reagan hoped to turn it into reality during the Star Wars programme of the 1980s, commonplace weapons remain, so far, perversely kinetic.

Research into new types of guns and beam weapons has initiated enormous changes in our world, even beyond the obvious effects that have been wrought by the actual use of guns. We have reviewed here some of these immense effects: on manufacture, on computing and artificial intelligence, and on geopolitics.

Reflecting on all the intellectual effort devoted to guns, or their possible replacements touched on in these pages, inevitably leads to a rather gloomy view of human creativity. The conclusion seems commonplace but inescapable that the greatest progress in technology occurs under the pressures of war or threatened wars. Perhaps one exception was the Moon race and the Apollo programme, which might be viewed

Artist's interpretation of the Raytheon 'pain beam'.

almost as a proxy, warlike competition. But could some other great challenge, perhaps a great and imminent danger such as the threat of global heating, evoke a similar range of inventions and creative thought?

EPILOGUE ON INVENTION

The last word goes to the pilot and writer Victor Yeates who flew 110 sorties in Sopwith Camels over the Western Front in 1918, was shot down twice and was credited with five victories. This was a pilot who, by the age of twenty, had an intimate knowledge of warfare and who became a powerful writer:

> The brains, thought Tom, of the Johnnies who invented the weapons of war! They invented an engine to drive a two-bladed air-screw at twelve hundred r.p.m. They invented a machine gun that would fire six hundred rounds in a minute, and when the inconvenience was felt of the propeller's masking the fire of the guns, a beneficial genius known as Constantinesco arose and made a gear that synchronised miraculously the absence of a blade with the presence of a bullet. It worked by oil pressure, and having taken a course, he was supposed to know all about it; but the fervid ingenuities of lethal genius were too much for his unmechanized brain. Within the past year, having never before approached nearer to mechanical operations than to clean a rifle, rewasher a tap, or maintain a push bicycle, he was supposed to have mastered the workings of several aero-engines, the Vickers gun and the Lewis gun, photography, the Morse code, aero-dynamics, bombs, the structure and rigging of sundry aeroplanes and the Constantinesco gear. He was also learning how to fly and how not to get shot down. But why didn't inventors confine their talents to inventing pleasant things? Anyone revising [Dante's] Inferno would have to make up a new worse-than-any circle for machine gun makers.[15]

REFERENCES

1 THE GEOMETRY OF WAR

1 N. I. Bukharin et al., *Science at the Crossroads: Papers Presented to the International Congress of the History of Science and Technology held in London from June 29th to July 3rd by the Delegates of the* U.S.S.R. (London, 1931). The publication of the papers was a great help to the dissemination of Hessen's ideas.

2 Boris Hessen, 'The Social and Economic Roots of Newton's Principia', ibid., pp. 150–212 (repr. London, 1971).

3 See Simon Ings, *Stalin and the Scientists: A History of Triumph and Tragedy, 1905–1953* (London, 2016).

4 Pope wrote the couplet as an epitaph for Newton's monument, although it was rejected. A much longer Latin text is used.

5 Simon Schaffer, 'Newton at the Crossroads', *Radical Philosophy*, RP 037 (Summer 1984). This version accessed at www.radicalphilosophyarchive. com.

6 Hessen, 'The Social and Economic Roots': 'On coming to power the bourgeoisie struggled mercilessly against the old guild and handicraft modes of production. With an iron hand it introduced large-scale machine industry, shattering in its course the resistance of the obsolete feudal class and the still unorganised protest of the new-born proletariat.'

7 Loren R. Graham, 'The Socio-political Roots of Boris Hessen: Soviet Marxism and the History of Science', *Social Studies of Science*, xv/4 (1985), pp. 705–22, suggests that there was a deeper meaning and Hessen's talk may also have been a subtle defence of Einstein's physics, then under attack in the Soviet Union. Ernst Kolman, the 'minder' of the group, had previously accused Hessen and other physicists of attempting to discredit materialism, calling them 'wreckers', recalling earlier industrial opponents of the revolution. Graham quotes Kolman, who wrote in 1931, 'The wreckers dare not say directly that they want to restore capitalism, they have to hide behind a convenient mask. And there is no more impenetrable mask . . . than a curtain of mathematical abstraction.'

8 Schaffer notes that 'Desmond Bernal, one of the leading communist scientists, wrote in 1939 that "we did not understand all they said, in fact, I now suspect they did not understand it entirely themselves, but we did recognise that there was something new and with immense possibilities of thought",' 'Newton at the Crossroads', p. 23.

9 See Ings, *Stalin and the Scientists*.

10 G. N. Clark, *Science and Social Welfare in the Age of Newton* (Oxford, 1937); review by D. McKie in *Annals of Science*, IV/1 (1939), p. 108.

11 A. Rupert Hall, *Ballistics in the Seventeenth Century* (Cambridge, 1952).

12 Frank James, 'The Springtime of Science: Modernity and the Future Past of Science', in *Being Modern: The Cultural Impact of Science in the Early Twentieth Century*, ed. Robert Bud, Paul Greenhalgh, Frank James and Morag Shiach (London, 2018), pp. 136, 137, 143. James suggests that this scholarly focus on seventeenth-century science, 'a regression back to the springtime of science', was, in part, impelled by the horrors of the Great War and the deployment of science in it. His subjects 'wished to see science as a force for good . . . shorn of any unfortunate connotations'.

13 Hall, *Ballistics*, p. 56.

14 Ibid. Hall asserted that Newton's science was too sophisticated to be useful for the gunners. Nor could the new manufacturing class 'use it to solve their crude practical problems' and it was only after 'engineering had transformed transport, manufacture and war in the early nineteenth century' that their problems became refined enough to need Newtonian mechanics. The guns of a First World War battleship are Newtonian machines, he inferred, but Cromwell's cannons were not. (Although the use of the word 'science' in relation to this period is sometimes thought anachronistic, it was used extensively in English to signify special knowledge of a range of studies including mathematics and mechanics.)

15 Tartaglia does seem to have conceded that the initial flight of the ball might be slightly curved, but his illustration does not show this. He seems to suggest that it is regarded as straight for practical purposes.

16 Hall, *Ballistics*. Among the works listed were John Roberts, *The Complete Cannoniere* (London 1639); *The Gunner, shewing the whole practice of Artillerie* (London, 1628); Samuel Sturmy, *The Mariner's Magazine; or, Sturmy's Mathematicall and Practicall Arts* (London, 1669).

17 Hall, *Ballistics*, p. 54, continued, 'some two hundred years later Nelson still held to this doctrine, observing "as to the plan of pointing a gun truer than we do at present, if the person comes I shall of course look at it and be happy, if necessary, to use it, but I hope we shall be able, as usual to get so close to our enemies that our shot cannot miss their object".'

18 Mary J. Henninger-Voss, 'How the "New Science" of Cannons Shook up the Aristotelian Cosmos', *Journal of the History of Ideas*, LXIII/3 (2002), pp. 371–97; quoted in Catherine Ann France, 'Gunnery and the Struggle for the New Science (1537–1687)', PhD thesis, University of Leeds, 2014, p. 26.

19 Robert Boyle, *Some Considerations touching the Usefulness of Natural Philosophy* (Oxford, 1664), quoted in Hall, *Ballistics*, p. 3.
20 Haileigh Robertson, '"Imitable Thunder": The Role of Gunpowder in Seventeenth-century Experimental Science', PhD thesis, University of York, 2015.
21 Henninger-Voss, 'How the "New Science" of Cannons'. Some historians have suggested that Simplicio was an unwise caricature of Pope Urban VIII (or that Urban VIII was persuaded by others that he was the intended subject).
22 France, 'Gunnery and the Struggle', p. 18. Digges had been tutored in mathematics by John Dee.
23 Ibid., p. 166. The parabolic theory is for an ideal projectile. Other factors, including air resistance, modify the path slightly and Galileo was aware of this.
24 Jean Buridan (*c.* 1300–*c.* 1360) is considered by modern writers to have anticipated the concepts of force and momentum ('the quantity of matter in a body multiplied by its velocity'), concepts on which Newton was to build.
25 France, 'Gunnery and the Struggle', pp. 16, 17.
26 More fully, The Royal Society of London for Improving Natural Knowledge.
27 Jim Bennett and Michael Hunter, *The Image of Restoration Science: The Frontispiece to Thomas Sprat's History of the Royal Society (1667)* (Abingdon, 2017), pp. 113–16.
28 Brouncker and, independently, Edme Mariotte in Paris, who experimented with different weights of projective, saw that the recoil was inversely related to the masses of the bullet and the weapon. (In other words, if the gun is fifty times heavier than the bullet it will recoil at 1/50th of the bullet's velocity.)
29 Hall, *Ballistics*, p. 65. Some prior 'Experiments for trying the force of great Guns by the learned Mr Greaves', originally dated 18 March 1651, were published in *Philosophical Transactions*, XV (1685), pp. 1090–92.
30 Jim Bennett and Stephen Johnston, *The Geometry of War, 1500–1750*, exh. cat., Museum of the History of Science, Oxford (Oxford, 1996).
31 Hessen's scrupulous reinterpretation of Newton in Marxist materialist terms was not enough to save him. He died in prison in Moscow in 1938. Six out of eight in the 1931 delegation were eliminated in the purges.
32 Steven Shapin, *Never Pure: Historical Studies of Science as if It Was Produced by People with Bodies, Situated in Time, Space, Culture, and Society, and Struggling for Credibility and Authority* (Baltimore, MD, 2010), is perhaps the most powerful recent exposition of these ideas.
33 From 'The General Scholium', the essay added to the second edition (1713) of Newton's *Principia Mathematica*; available at http://isaac-newton.org, accessed 4 May 2020.

34 This passage was studied in the final paragraph of Bennett and Johnston's
    The Geometry of War, from where the quotation is drawn.

2 THE GUN AND THE FORD

1   Ken Alder, 'Engineering Rationality and Interchangeable Parts', *Technology
    and Culture*, XXXVIII/3 (1997), pp. 273–311.
2   Ibid.
3   The prospectus for the *Encyclopédie ou dictionnaire raisonné des sciences, des
    arts et des métiers* was issued in 1750 and volumes were published in France
    between 1751 and 1772, with numerous later supplements and additions.
    The work seemed so contentious that, for a while, publication was stopped
    and Jean le Rond d'Alembert abandoned the project. A great part of the
    Encyclopédie therefore is the work of Diderot.
4   Extracts from the entries on 'Encyclopedia' and 'Art' from the *Encyclopédie*
    (1751–72) by Denis Diderot; Eng. trans. available at 'The Encyclopedia of
    Diderot and d'Alembert', https://quod.lib.umich.edu, accessed 14 June
    2019.
5   Ibid.
6   Alder, 'Engineering Rationality', pp. 300–305.
7   John Houghton, *Collection of Letters* (London, 1681), p. 177; quoted in
    E. P. Thompson, 'Time, Work-discipline and Industrial Capitalism',
    Past and Present, 38 (1967), p. 72.
8   Ibid., p. 73.
9   Ibid.
10 John Foster, *An Essay on the Evils of Popular Ignorance* (London, 1821),
    p. 185; quoted in Thompson, 'Time, Work-discipline and Industrial
    Capitalism', p. 90.
11 Clive Behagg, 'Mass Production without the Factory: Craft Producers,
    Guns and Small Firm Innovation, 1790–1815', *Business History*, XL/3 (1998),
    pp. 1–15.
12 Adam Smith, from an early draft of *The Wealth of Nations*; quoted in
    Simon Schaffer, 'Enlightened Automata', in *The Sciences in Enlightened
    Europe*, ed. W. Clark, J. Golinski and S. Schaffer (Chicago, IL, 1999),
    p. 130.
13 The Italian Renaissance too spawned imaginative thinkers in theoretical
    engineering, such as Leonardo da Vinci, although it is often asserted that
    his ideas had little effect on practical contemporary machine builders.
    For a discussion of the organic, vernacular evolution of medieval and
    early modern mechanisms, see John Gimpel, *The Medieval Machine:
    The Industrial Revolution of the Middle Ages* (London, 1992).
14 Behagg, 'Mass Production without the Factory'. The jewellery quarter
    in Birmingham had remarkable and timely support from English Heritage
    which has preserved many important structures. In London, many of the

old buildings that housed this craft production also survived, although now are completely repurposed. However, because they grew in an organic and ad hoc way, these sites no longer speak of their old industries.

15 Report from the Select Committee on the Manufacture of Small Arms (P.P. 1854, xviii, 12), Q.1662; quoted in Behagg, 'Mass Production without the Factory'.

16 Behagg, 'Mass Production without the Factory'.

17 John Rule, *The Labouring Classes in Early Industrial England, 1750–1850* (London, 2013), pp. 81–139. See also *A History of the County of Warwick*, vol. VII: *The City of Birmingham*, Victoria County History (London, 1964); available at British History Online, www.british-history.ac.uk, accessed 5 May 2020.

18 Alder, 'Engineering Rationality and Interchangeable Parts', p. 283.

19 Report from the Select Committee on the Manufacture of Small Arms, quoted in Behagg, 'Mass Production without the Factory'.

20 In terms of economic demand, the populations of Britain and the United States were roughly equal at this time. However, it is certainly true that expansion and settlement into the USA created a huge number of new households and a market for new goods that could be met by standardized products.

21 George Sturt, *The Wheelwright's Shop* (Cambridge, 1923) is a notable attempt. The work is a poignant evocation of English rural hand craft at the end of the nineteenth century. In this world tacit knowledge was all. Timber was often chosen while it was still a growing tree and the wood seasoned for years. But even his elegiac prose cannot lead the reader close to being able to select wood for a spoke or a wheel hub by eye and feel, or to sense the quality of a piece of elm in the spring of his chisel.

22 David A. Hounshell, *From the American System to Mass Production, 1800–1932: The Development of Manufacturing Technology in the United States* (Baltimore, MD, 1984). This must be the most complete historical study of the evolution of this system.

23 Ibid.

24 Ibid.

25 James P. Womack, Daniel T. Jones and Daniel Roos, *The Machine that Changed the World* (New York, 1990).

26 Charles E. Sorensen, *My Forty Years with Ford* (New York, 1956), p. 128.

27 Henry Ford, *My Life and Work* (Garden City, NY, 1922), p. 2.

28 Julian Sweet, quoted by A. L. Kennedy in 'Production Line Living', BBC Radio 3, 27 October 2013.

29 Andrew Nahum, 'A Roof With a View: Fiat's Lingotto', *Weekend Guardian*, 22–3 April 1989, p. 6.

30 Horace Lucien Arnold and Fay Leone Faurote, *Ford Methods and the Ford Shops* (New York, 1919). After Arnold's death the work was finished by the engineer Fay Leone Faurote.

31 See Cesare De Seta, *L'architettura del Novecento* (Turin, 1981); referenced in Terry Kirk, *The Architecture of Modern Italy*, vol. II: *Visions of Utopia, 1900–Present* (New York, 2005); see also 'Giacomo Matté-Trucco', www.architetturafuturista.it, accessed 6 May 2020, and Andrew Nahum, 'The Italian Job', *Blueprint*, December 1984–January 1985, p. 24.

32 Curiously, although Italy was one of the first nations to deploy Fordism in its most literal guise, it also held on to the tradition of handwork and bespoke design with its tradition of special high-performance cars and motorcycles, produced in small numbers, but with a high price and reputation. Ferrari, Lamborghini, Maserati, MV Agusta, Moto Guzzi and Ducati all owe their origins and continuance to this extraordinary Italian gift, as does the emergence of organizations like Pininfarina and Giorgetto Giugiaro's Italdesign as creative design consultants to the world's auto industry over many decades.

33 Terry Kirk, *The Architecture of Modern Italy*, 2 vols (New York, 2005), vol. II, p. 61.

34 Nelson Lichtenstein, *Walter Reuther: The Most Dangerous Man in Detroit* (Chicago, IL, 1995), p. 17.

35 Ford estimated that the retooling costs were around $100 million. Later analysts think this was an underestimate. In addition, 60,000 production workers shared the cost by being laid off when the lines closed for six months. See, for example, Giles Slade, *Made to Break: Technology and Obsolescence in America* (Cambridge, MA, 2007).

36 'Men Working to Keep Men Working', *Life* (7 November 1949).

37 'A car for every purse and purpose' was how Alfred P. Sloan, at the helm of General Motors, described his market segmentation strategy in a 1924 report to stockholders. It was a distinctly different philosophy to Ford's.

38 Slade, *Made to Break*, p. 46.

39 Womack, Jones and Roos, *The Machine that Changed the World*.

40 David E. Nye, *America's Assembly Line* (Cambridge, MA, 2013); and Kim Moody, 'American Labor in International Lean Production', Institute for Social Science Research, UCLA, Working Paper Series qt21j3p024 (1996); available at https://escholarship.org, accessed 6 May 2020.

41 Malcolm Moore, 'Inside Foxconn's Suicide Factory', *Daily Telegraph*, 27 May 2010. See also Joel Johnson, '1 Million Workers. 90 Million iPhones. 17 Suicides. Who's to Blame?', *Wired*, 28 February 2011, www.wired.com, accessed 6 May 2020.

42 Chuck Quirmbach, 'Foxconn Promised 13,000 Jobs to Wisconsin. Where Are They?', NPR, 13 January 2020, www.npr.org, accessed 6 May 2020.

43 Schaffer, 'Enlightened Automata', pp. 126–64.

44 Adam Ferguson, 'Part Fourth, Of Consequences that result from the Advancement of Civil and Commercial Arts', *An Essay on the History of Civil Society* (London and Edinburgh, 1767); available at *Online Library of Liberty*, https://oll.libertyfund.org, accessed 6 May 2020.

3 THE GODFATHER OF OIL

1 Osbert Sitwell, *Great Morning* (London, 1948), p. 229. Though Sitwell's
   undoubtedly gilded London circle included the opera singer Feodor
   Chaliapin, Vaslav Nijinsky and Sergei Diaghilev of the Ballets Russes,
   Richard Strauss, Frederick Delius and Henry James, he also observed the
   Liberal government's new programme of social reform, and its introduction
   of old age pensions and social insurance schemes.
2 Winston Churchill, *The World Crisis, 1911–1918* [1923–9], revd edn, 2 vols
   (London, 1938), p. 86.
3 Winston Churchill, *Great Contemporaries* (London, 1942), p. 30.
4 Lord Fisher [Admiral Sir John Arbuthnot Fisher], *Memories* (London,
   1919), p. 23.
5 Ibid., p. 36.
6 There was also a rival gunnery control machine, the Argo Clock, devised
   by Arthur Pollen. The choice of Dreyer's system gave rise to much
   acrimony and post-war controversy.
7 Andrew Gordon, *The Rules of the Game: Jutland and British Naval
   Command* (London, 2005), p. 120.
8 Charles Parsons was an early and intuitive exponent of house style
   and the idea of consistent branding. Intuitively sensing that the
   phrase 'Charles Parsons's steam turbine' was inherently ugly, he
   issued a company-wide decree that the device was always to be called 'the
   Parsons steam turbine'.
9 Christopher Leyland, 'Turbinia Jottings', *Heaton Works Journal*, 11/1 (June
   1935), pp. 25–32, quoted in Ian Whitehead, '"Turbinia" at speed – but who's
   on the conning tower?', Tyne & Wear Archives & Museums blog, 13 June
   2013, http://blog.twmuseums.org.uk, accessed 12 May 2020. An interesting
   legacy of Christopher Leyland is the controversial cypress *Cupressus* x
   Leylandii. He found, on his estate, that he had produced accidental hybrids
   between the Californian Monterey cypress and an Alaskan Nootka cypress.
   These parent species could never have 'met' in the wild and could only have
   propagated through the agency of a keen tree collector and gardener. They
   proved extraordinarily vigorous and hardy enough to withstand the wind at
   his Northumberland home.
10 Churchill, *The World Crisis*, vol. 1, pp. 57, 58.
11 Ibid., p. 97.
12 Ibid., p. 95.
13 Ibid., p. 100.
14 Ibid., p. 104.
15 Eli Kedouri, *Arab Political Memoirs and Other Studies* (Oxford, 2005),
   p. 275.
16 See Jonathan Fenby, *Crucible: Thirteen Months that Forged Our World*
   (London, 2018).

17 'Orde Charles Wingate – "Hayedid"', available at https://zionism-israel.
    com, accessed 26 November 2020.
18 This has been discussed by many participants in the battle as well as in
    numerous historical works. See for example John Brooks, *Dreadnought
    Gunnery and the Battle of Jutland: The Development of Fire-control*
    (Oxford, 2005).
19 Beatty's remark was an echo of Nelson's second signal at Trafalgar: 'engage
    the enemy more closely', but seems to have given away a great advantage
    that his ships had. He should, it has been argued, have fired on and struck
    Hipper's ships powerfully, while remaining out of range of their shells.
20 *The Beatty Papers*, ed. B. Mcl. Ranft, vol. ii, document 233 (Navy Records
    Society, 1993), p. 451, available at www.gwpda.org, accessed 24 November
    2020. Hipper added, 'If the English did not attain greater results, it is on
    account of the bad quality of their shell, particularly with reference to the
    insufficient efficiency of their [explosives].'
21 Rodrigo Garcia y Robertson, 'The Failure of the Heavy Gun at Sea,
    1898–1922', *Technology and Culture*, 28 (1987), pp. 539–57.

4 HIGH PHEASANTS IN THEORY AND PRACTICE

1 Major Sir Gerald Burrard, *The Modern Shotgun* (London, 1931).
2 Burrard had to admit priority, following a report in *The Field* (20
   September 1890), to 'the first person to have conducted any experiments on
   this line . . . Mr H. A. Ivatt, who fired a few shots . . . at an iron target fixed
   to a railway train'. This opportunity was, unusually, available to Ivatt as one
   of Britain's leading designers of steam locomotives and then chief engineer
   at the Great Southern and Western Railway in Ireland.
3 The murder of Zemenides was never solved. He had a more complex
   life than initial facts suggested. Described as a leader of the Cypriot
   community in London, he had formed a Christian Cypriot nationalist
   (and anti-Communist) association. The *Daily Worker* described him as
   'a notorious imperialist', while the *Daily Express* quoted rumours that
   he was a (British) secret service agent. He was also described as a police
   informer.
4 Sir Ralph Payne-Gallwey, Bart, *High Pheasants in Theory and Practice*
   (London, 1913).
5 Ibid., pp. 1–8.
6 There is, however, a report that Lieutenant O.F.J. Hogg and the No. 2
   AA Section, Royal Garrison Artillery, shot down an aircraft in France on
   23 September 1914; see N. W. Routledge, *History of the Royal Regiment of
   Artillery*, vol. iv: *Anti-Aircraft Artillery, 1914–55* (London, 1994), p. 5.
7 Victor Yeates, *Winged Victory* (London, 1934), pp. 20, 21. The words are
   actually put in the mouth of Yeates's protagonist Tom Cundall, although
   the events are the intense experiences of Yeates himself.

8 Sir Alfred Rawlinson, *The Defence of London, 1915–1918*, 2nd edn (London, 1923). Rawlinson commented, 'The dropping of these extremely inefficient bombs, however, did infinitely more good than harm and vastly increased our chances of emerging victorious from the great struggle in which we had engaged' (p. 4).

9 Admiral Sir Percy Scott, *Fifty Years in the Royal Navy* (London, 1919), pp. 309–10.

10 Rawlinson, *Defence of London*, p. 3. Rawlinson had good contacts in France with Generals Gallieni and Joffre, spoke good French and had helped plan anti-aircraft defences around Paris.

11 Scott, *Fifty Years in the Royal Navy*, pp. 309–11. According to Scott, 'That is the sort of officer that is wanted in wartime!'

12 'The Anti-Aircraft Experimental Section of the Munitions Inventions Department' (1916–18). Draft memoir in the archives of Churchill College, Cambridge. A variant of these memoirs appears in A. V. Hill, *Memories and Reflections*, ed. Roger Thomas (1971/2), available at www.chu.cam.ac.uk, accessed 14 May 2020.

13 Ian V. Hogg, *Barrage* (London, 1979), p. 95.

14 A. V. Hill papers, note in Churchill College archives, Cambridge.

15 G. H. Hardy, *A Mathematician's Apology* [1940] (Cambridge, 1996), p. 140.

16 'The Anti-Aircraft Experimental Section of the Munitions Inventions Department'.

17 Meg Weston Smith, 'E. A. Milne and the Creation of Air Defence: Some Letters from an Unprincipled Brigand, 1916–1919', *Notes and Records: Royal Society Journal of the History of Science*, XLIV/2 (1990), pp. 241–55.

18 A. V. Hill papers, Churchill College archives.

19 Bernard Katz, 'Archibald Vivian Hill', *Biographical Memoirs of Fellows of the Royal Society*, XXIV (November 1978), pp. 71–149.

20 The Central Register was formally administered by the Ministry of Labour and headed by the pioneering female civil servant Beryl le Poer Power, who had a reputation as an exceptionally forceful individual. The novelist and Cambridge academic C. P. Snow was a member of the team and active in interviewing and assigning scientists.

21 Sir Bernard Lovell, F.R.S, 'Patrick Maynard Stuart Blackett, Baron Blackett, of Chelsea', *Biographical Memoirs of Fellows of the Royal Society* (1 November 1975), p. 56.

22 Sir Bernard Lovell, 'Patrick Maynard Stuart Blackett', *Biographical Memoirs of Fellows of the Royal Society*, XXI (1975), pp. 1–115.

23 Ibid.

24 E. Austin Young, *How We Lived and Laughed (with the 195)* (n.p., 1945), printed for the 61st Heavy Anti-aircraft Regiment.

5 FIRE CONTROL AND A NEW SCIENCE OF LIFE

1 Kazimierz Bortkiewicz, *8 Polish Heavy Anti-aircraft Artillery Regiment: The Outlines of History* (London, 1993).

2 Perhaps only half of these, or fewer, were downed by anti-aircraft gunnery, with the rest falling victim to American aircraft or to accident.

3 The Radiation Laboratory had been set up by the National Defense Research Committee under the chairmanship of Vannevar Bush and was one of the NDRC's biggest projects.

4 David A. Mindell, 'Automation's Finest Hour: Radar and System Integration in World War II', in *Systems, Experts, and Computers: The Systems Approach in Management and Engineering, World War II and After*, ed. Agatha C. Hughes and Thomas P. Hughes (Cambridge, MA, 2000).

5 Wiener is said to have derived the new word from the classical Greek term for steersman or pilot, although the term *cybernétique*, to describe the art of governing, had been used in France in the nineteenth century.

6 Norbert Wiener, *The Human Use of Human Beings* (London, 1950), p. 163. Wiener was almost certainly talking from personal experience. He had notably bad eyesight and severe cataracts.

7 Bertrand Russell, letter to Lucy Donnelly, 19 October 1913, quoted in Maria Forte, 'Bertrand Russell's letters to Helen Thomas Flexner and Lucy Martin Donnelly', PhD thesis, McMaster University, December 1988, p. 209.

8 Flo Conway and Jim Siegelman, *Dark Hero of the Information Age: In Search of Norbert Wiener* (Cambridge, MA, 2005), p. 30.

9 Arturo Rosenblueth, Norbert Wiener and Julian Bigelow, 'Behavior, Purpose and Teleology', *Philosophy of Science*, X (1943), pp. 18–24.

10 Wiener, *The Human Use of Human Beings*.

11 Norbert Wiener, *Cybernetics; or, Control and Communication in the Animal and the Machine* (Paris and Cambridge, MA, 1948).

12 Wiener, *The Human Use of Human Beings*, pp. 85, 88.

13 N. Katherine Hales, *How We Became Post-human: Virtual Bodies in Cybernetics, Literature and Informatics* (Chicago, IL, 1999), p. xi.

14 See, for example, Soraya de Chadarevian, *Designs for Life: Molecular Biology after World War II* (Cambridge, 2002), p. 188.

15 Lily Kay, *Who Wrote the Book of Life?: A History of the Genetic Code* (Stanford, CA, 2000), p. 34 and elsewhere.

16 The challenge of understanding how DNA worked spawned useful terms like transcription, translation and messenger RNA. The spread of information language has been irresistible.

17 Warren S. McCulloch, 'Recollections of the Many Sources of Cybernetics', *ASC Forum*, VI/2 (Summer 1974), pp. 5–16.

18 Ibid.

19 Quoted in Margaret A. Boden, *Mind as Machine: A History of Cognitive Science* (Oxford, 2006), p. vi.

20 Ibid.

21 Andrew Pickering, *The Cybernetic Brain: Sketches of Another Future*
    (Chicago, IL, 2011). Although Kenneth Craik (1914–1945) was characterized
    as 'the British Wiener', he was a more modest figure. It is unlikely, had
    he lived, that he would have defined and proselytized for the new field
    of cybernetics in the way that Wiener was destined to do.

22 From the J.A.V. Bates archive, The Wellcome Library for the History
    and Understanding of Medicine, quoted in Owen Holland, 'Early
    British Cybernetics and the Ratio Club', 31st Annual Conference of the
    Cybernetics Society (London, 2006). Rev. as Owen Holland and Phil
    Husbands, 'The Origins of British Cybernetics: the Ratio Club', *Kybernetes*,
    XL (2011), pp. 110–23. In another note, Bates mused on the membership:
    'No Sociologists, Northerners, Professors'.

23 Ibid. See also Phil Husbands and Owen Holland, 'Warren McCulloch
    and the British Cyberneticians', *Interdisciplinary Science Reviews*, 3 (2012),
    pp. 237–53.

24 Phil Husbands and Owen Holland, 'The Ratio Club: A Hub of British
    Cybernetics', in *The Mechanical Mind in History*, ed. Phil Husbands, Owen
    Holland and Michael Wheeler (Cambridge, MA, 2008), pp. 91–148.

25 Ibid., p. 14.

26 Holland and Husbands, 'The Origins of British Cybernetics', p. 39.

27 See Andrew Hodges, *Alan Turing: The Enigma* (London, 2014), pp. 561–2,
    and Grey Walter, *The Living Brain* (London and New York, 1953).

28 Rhodri Hayward, 'The Tortoise and the Love-Machine: Grey Walter and
    the Politics of Electroencephalography', *Science in Context*, XIV/4 (2001),
    p. 616.

29 Grey Walter, *The Living Brain* (London, 1961), p. 83.

30 Ibid., p. 129.

31 Ibid., p. 112.

32 Pierre de Latil, *Thinking by Machine*, trans. Y. M. Golla (London, 1956),
    pp. 208–14. De Latil is quoted at length here because his visits to the
    cyberneticians themselves captured the spirit of the times so well.

33 Ibid., pp. 213–14.

34 The Cambridge radio astronomer Tony Hewish recalled of his time in
    wartime radar research that 'our stuff was just thrown together . . . the
    war was a race, and we were better at that than the Germans'; conversation
    with the author, Churchill College, Cambridge, 11 October 2012.

35 Husbands and Holland, in *The Mechanical Mind in History*, p. 114.

36 *Daily Herald*, 13 December 1948, quoted in Pickering, *The Cybernetic Brain*,
    p. 1.

37 Pickering, *The Cybernetic Brain*, p. 93.

38 G.W.T.H. Fleming, F. L. Golla and W. Grey Walter, 'Electric Convulsion
    Therapy of Schizophrenia', *The Lancet* (30 December 1939), pp. 1352–5. The
    experiment would certainly not be regarded as ethical today and the authors

noted that 'this small preliminary series was not intended to provide data on the therapeutic value of the treatment – in only one of the patients could a remission be hoped for with any confidence – but was designed to throw light on the relative advantages and dangers of the method.'

39 Wiener, 'Cybernetics and Psychopathology', *Cybernetics*, pp. 144–54.

40 Ibid.

41 Ibid.

42 Pickering, *Cybernetic Brain*, p. 133.

43 From Ross Ashby's unpublished journal, analysed by Andrew Pickering, *Cybernetic Brain*, pp. 140–43. Pickering also points out that Ashby had been reading Clausewitz's *On War*.

44 Latil, *Thinking by Machine*, p. 310.

45 Ibid., p. 311.

46 Ibid.

47 The Milk Marketing Board did not finally lose its remaining powers until 1994.

48 Andy Beckett, 'Santiago Dreaming', *The Guardian,* 8 September 2003.

49 BBC archive, BBC WAC T14/3316/1. In fact, the date and authorship are surmises although probable. Nor was the programme yet called *Horizon*: Quest, Crucible, Prospect and Scan were other candidate titles.

50 This is still a contentious area. To 'know everything' an AI system needs to have values and information for everything in its frame or problem, and represent them symbolically. In recent years, Rodney Brooks, MIT researcher and robotics entrepreneur, has argued that this degree of complex processing simply cannot be what is going on in animal and human performance and that there must be solutions to responsive or intelligent action that are more computationally economical.

51 'Edinburgh Freddy Robot (Mid 1960s to 1981)', www.aiai.ed.ac.uk, accessed 16 May 2020.

52 Jack Good, lecture at the Department of Machine Intelligence, University of Edinburgh, *c.* 1972, author's recollection.

53 In the words of one member of the department, Good's cricketer example would have been 'music to Donald's ears'. Personal communication from David Willshaw, Emeritus Professor of Computational Neurobiology, School of Informatics, University of Edinburgh. Willshaw had been a PhD student in the department during this period.

54 See, for example, Patricia Churchland, *Neurophilosophy* (Cambridge, MA, 1986), and Patricia Churchland, 'Can Neurobiology Teach Us Anything about Consciousness?', *Proceedings and Addresses of the American Philosophical Association*, LXVII/4 (1994), pp. 23–40.

55 In fact, it could not always achieve this. Cleverly, the programmers arranged for Freddy to knock the heap of parts around with the pincer until they fell into orientations that matched its stored model.

56 Hubert L. Dreyfus, RAND Corporation, P-3244, December 1965. According

to Dreyfus, after his attack his colleagues working at MIT in AI 'dared not be seen having lunch with [him]' following publication of his paper. He remained uncowed, however, and followed up the RAND paper with his book *What Computers Still Can't Do: A Critique of Artificial Reason* (Cambridge, MA, 1972).

57 At the time of writing the complete debate is available on YouTube under the title 'The Lighthill Debate on Artificial Intelligence'. The formal Lighthill Report itself, at the time of writing, is available at www.chilton-computing.org.uk.

58 Kevin Kelly, *Out of Control: The Rise of Neo-biological Civilization* (Reading, MA, 1994), p. 454; quoted in Thomas Rid, *Rise of the Machines: A Cybernetic History* (New York, 2016), p. 165.

59 Grey Walter wrote movingly about his emergence from a month of coma following the accident and his brain injuries in the article 'My Miracle', *Theoria to Theory*, VI/2 (April 1972), pp. 39–50; available at http://cyberneticzoo.com and www.hathitrust.org, both accessed 16 May 2020.

60 Alan Winfield, 'Artificial Intelligence', *The Infinite Monkey Cage*, BBC Radio 4, 12 January 2016.

6 COWBOYS, COLTS AND KALASHNIKOVS

1 Although the term 'Native American' is now in common use, it is not universal among the indigenous peoples of North America, the 'first nations'. For example, the National Museum of the American Indian in Washington, DC, opened in 2004, was so named after extensive consultation with the peoples whose cultures it represents. In this text, the term 'Indian' is generally used where the 'Native American' would be anachronistic, and particularly in historical references.

2 Although the Great Plains Indians had lived by hunting buffalo, the stocks were stable. The first threat came with the building of the railroads. Before he became a showman, Buffalo Bill had a contract to supply the workers building the Kansas-Pacific railroad with meat. By the 1870s buffalo hunting for sport was systematic and encouraged by the belief that exterminating the buffalo would reduce the Indian population or force them to become settled smallholders.

3 Melvyn Bragg in 'Custer's Last Stand', *In Our Time*, BBC Radio 4, 19 May 2011. The quotation comes from a Lakota warrior via oral tradition.

4 Some sources suggest that these were Hotchkiss machine guns – early automatic weapons with rotating barrels. However, the weapons seem to have been the type of small cannon that could be broken down for carriage by mule.

5 John Gneisenau Neihardt, *Black Elk Speaks: Being the Life Story of a Holy Man of the Oglala Sioux* [1932] (Albany, NY, 2008), p. 281. The Oglala are one of the seven groups that make up the Lakota division of the Great Sioux Nation.

6 Jan Morris, *Fisher's Face* (London, 1995), p. 197.
7 Wild West shows were big business and there were many imitators. One
   intriguing u.s. showman in Britain was Samuel Franklin Cody with his
   own show, *The Klondyke Nugget*. (He had changed his name from Cowdery
   for commercial reasons.) Marksmanship and horsemanship were again big
   features, with Cody (apparently) shooting a cigarette from the lips of his
   partner Lela, as he galloped round. Remarkably, he developed an interest
   in huge man-carrying kites, which he developed for army reconnaissance.
   He was adopted by the army Balloon School at Farnborough (later the
   Royal Aircraft Establishment) and eventually achieved the first powered
   aeroplane flight in Britain in 1908 with a machine of his own design.
8 Eric Vuillard, *Sitting Bull and the Tragedy of Show Business*, trans. Ann
   Jefferson (London, 2016), gives a far more sceptical reading of the Wild
   West show, characterizing the celebrated photograph of Sitting Bull and
   Cody shaking hands as a cynical photo opportunity, remarking that 'At that
   time, Buffalo Bill . . . was already a pure product of marketing, a sort of
   sham.'
9 Patricia Allen, 'Glasgow's *Ghost Dance* Shirt: Reflections on a Circuit to
   Complete', in *Global Ancestors: Understanding the Shared Humanity of
   Our Ancestors*, ed. Margaret Clegg, Rebecca Redfern, Jelena Bekvalac
   and Heather Bonney (Oxford, 2013), pp. 63–80. Allen describes the details
   of the original acquisition and the repatriation negotiations with the
   representatives of the Lakota people.
10 William B. Edwards, *The Story of Colt's Revolver* (Harrisburg, PA, 1953),
   p. 23.
11 Ibid., p. 268.
12 *Official Descriptive and Illustrated Catalogue*, III: *Foreign States* (London,
   1851), p. 1454.
13 Report from the Select Committee on the Manufacture of Small Arms
   (P.P. 1854, XVIII, 12), Q.1662; quoted in Clive Behagg, 'Mass Production
   without the Factory: Craft Producers, Guns and Small Firm Innovation,
   1790–1815', *Business History*, XL/3 (1998), pp. 1–15.
14 Jenni Calder, *There Must be a Lone Ranger: The Myth and Reality of the
   American West* (London, 1976), p. 6.
15 Walter Huston played the Wyatt Earp character in *Law and Order* and
   his son John Huston contributed to the screenplay.
16 Calder, *There Must be a Lone Ranger*, p. 109.
17 Jonny Wilkes, 'The Gunfight at OK Corral', *History Revealed* (2014), p. 84.
18 Lord Charles Beresford, *The Memoirs of Admiral Lord Charles Beresford:
   Written by Himself* (London, 1914), vol. I, pp. 262–5. There were
   geometrical reasons for the weakness of the rear corners. Unlike a frontal
   assault, which is met by the full fire of the front ranks, a cavalry charge
   slanting down towards a rear corner can attack men who blanket the fire
   of their comrades behind them.

19 Ibid.

20 Ibid.

21 Ibid.

22 Ibid., vol. II, p. 277.

23 The title is a phrase taken from a poem by Lucretius: 'the torch of life'.
    The square at Abu Klea, though briefly penetrated, reformed and held.
    In the days when those infantry tactics reigned it seems that no British
    square was ever truly broken.

24 Beresford, *The Memoirs of Admiral Lord Charles Beresford: Written by
    Himself*, pp. 267–8.

25 Hiram Maxim, *My Life* (London, 1915), p. 57.

26 Ibid.

27 Ibid.

28 Dennis E. Showalter and Michael S. Neiberg, *The Nineteenth Century*
    (Westport, CT, 2006), p. 146.

29 Hiram Maxim, 'The Aeroplane', *Cosmopolitan* (June 1892), pp. 202–8.
    The pioneer aeronautical thinker Francis Wenham also supported the
    view that Maxim intended to fly the machine, noting in a letter to Octave
    Chanute in May 1895 that 'He has shown that the machine will raise its
    own weight with several persons . . . yet no one will dare to venture on a
    free flight,' and subsequently, 'Maxim has spent many hundreds of pounds
    . . . but if no one can be found who will undertake to fly away in his
    finished machine, there is the end of it'; Pearl I. Young, *Chanute–Wenham
    Correspondence* (Lancaster, PA, 1964).

30 C. J. Chivers, *The Gun: The AK-47 and the Evolution of War* (New York and
    London, 2010), p. 192.

31 No one seems to know the origin of the term 'round' for a unit of
    ammunition: the cartridge casing, a primer, propellant (the 'powder')
    and the bullet. Some suggest that it is army usage because these items are
    cylindrical. Others suggest that in the days of muzzle loaders the process
    of charging the musket sequentially with powder, wadding and bullet
    was called 'a round', like the sequence of movements in an old-time dance.

32 Eugene Stoner explained the effect this way to the congressional
    subcommittee on small arms: 'There is the advantage that a small or light
    bullet has over a heavy one when it comes to wound ballistics . . . What
    it amounts to is the fact that bullets are stabilized to fly through the air,
    and not through water, or a body, which is approximately the same density
    as the water. And they are stable as long as they are in the air. When they
    hit something, they immediately go unstable . . . If you are talking about
    .30-caliber [like the larger bullet used in the older M-14], this might remain
    stable through a human body . . . While a little bullet, being it has a low
    mass, it senses an instability situation faster and reacts much faster . . . this
    is what makes a little bullet pay off so much in wound ballistics.' Quoted
    in James Fallows, 'M-16: A Bureaucratic Horror Story: Why the Rifles

Jammed', in *National Defense* (Washington, DC, 1981); repr. in *The Atlantic* (June 1981), available at www.theatlantic.com, accessed 18 May 2020.

33 Sullivan said, 'The M16 system was functioning just right, but when the powder was changed, the gas port pressure that operates the gas system that operates the bolt had much higher pressure. It made the bolt move faster than it was designed for, and it began unlocking too early, which put stresses on the locking lugs. Also, the cartridge metal hadn't relaxed in the chamber enough, particularly when the weapon got hot, and the cartridge would stick in there, keeping the extractor from extracting the cartridge.' Dan L. Shea, 'The Interview: James L. Sullivan', *Small Arms Review*, 11/6 (March 2008).

34 Chivers, *The Gun: The AK-47 and the Evolution of War*, p. 269.

35 Ibid., p. 401.

36 Virginia Ezell, 'Obituary: Eugene Stoner', *Independent Online*, 30 May 1992.

37 Chivers, *The Gun: The AK-47 and the Evolution of War*.

38 A few months before his death, aged 94, Kalashnikov did apparently have more sombre thoughts. He had converted to the Russian Orthodox Church and in 2012, two years before his death, wrote a letter to the Patriarch. Published in *Izvestia*, this confessed that 'the pain in my soul is unbearable. I keep asking myself the same unsolvable question: If my assault rifle took people's lives, it means that I, Mikhail Kalashnikov . . . son of a farmer and Orthodox Christian, am responsible for people's deaths . . . The longer I live, the deeper I go in my thoughts and guesses about why the Almighty allowed humans to have devilish desires of envy, greed and aggression.' See Jim Heintz, 'Kalashnikov dies: "I sleep well," said the designer of the AK-47', *Christian Science Monitor*, 23 December 2013.

39 There is the intriguing case of the Japanese rejection of gun warfare. Some sources suggest that prior to 1588 many Japanese warlords each had more firearms than entire European states. Thereafter guns were abandoned for some two hundred years, perhaps, according to one writer, because the Samurai class valued 'the skill, strength, grace and courage required to use the sword'. By implication, they resented dying at the hands of a 'commoner . . . wielding a gun from a "cowardly" distance'. By some form of collective sense, Samurai stopped using guns against each other (though they retained them for hunting) and suppressed their use by those below them in social ranking. This disposition ended with the arrival of Commodore Perry and his warship in 1854.

40 This exchange, it is said, occurred when curator Edward Ezell of the Smithsonian brought the two together to discuss their weapons for an oral history project in 1990.

7 FROM DEATH RAYS TO STAR WARS

1 H. G. Wells, *The War of the Worlds* (New York, 1898), pp. 34–6.
2 See Chapter Four. In the First World War A. V. Hill had been instrumental in putting anti-aircraft gunnery on a scientific footing.
3 Wimperis was also a member of the Tizard Committee, set up to explore all conceivable means of defence against bombers. Although a beam weapon was not possible, he reported that Watson-Watt's consoling response was that 'attention is being turned to the still difficult, but less unpromising, problem of radio detection as opposed to radio destruction'; *Formation of a Scientific Committee on Air Defence*, File AIR 2/4481/ S34763 (minutes of 12 November 1934), National Archives, Kew, London. The brief of the committee was to study 'how far recent advances in scientific and technical knowledge can be used to strengthen the present methods of defence against hostile aircraft'.
4 Peter J. Westwick, 'From the Club of Rome to Star Wars: The Era of Limits, Space Colonization and the Origins of SDI', in *Limiting Outer Space: Astroculture after Apollo*, ed. Alexander C. T. Geppert (London, 2018), pp. 283–302; see also review by Jeff Foust, *Space Review*, 30 July 2018.
5 Peter Goodchild, *Edward Teller: The Real Dr Strangelove* (London, 2004), p. 347; Donald R. Baucom, *The Origins of SDI, 1941–1983* (Lawrence, KS, 1992), p. 189.
6 Edward Teller, with Judith Schoolery, *Memoirs* (New York, 2001), pp. 529, 530.
7 'The Conclusion of President Reagan's March 23, 1983, Speech on Defense Spending and Defensive Technology', *Arms Control in Outer Space: Hearings before the Subcommittee on International Security and Scientific Affairs* (Washington, DC, 1984), pp. 344–5.
8 John Lewis Gaddis, *The Cold War* (London, 2005), pp. 224–8.
9 William E. Pemberton, *Exit with Honor: The Life and Presidency of Ronald Reagan*, The Right Wing in America (Armonk, NY, 1997), p. 156.
10 Michael R. Fitzgerald and Allen Packwood, eds, *Out of the Cold: The Cold War and Its Legacy* (London, 2013), pp. 39–52. The work is the record of the conference 'The Cold War and Its Legacy', hosted by Churchill College, Cambridge, 18–19 November 2009.
11 William E. Pemberton, *Exit with Honour: The Life and Presidency of Ronald Reagan* (Oxford and New York, 2015), p. 132.
12 See C. J. Chivers, *The Gun: The AK-47 and the Evolution of War* (New York and London, 2010).
13 Quoted in Sarah Bridger, *Scientists at War: The Ethics of Cold War Weapons Research* (Cambridge, MA, 2015), p. 245.
14 This account does not deal here with 'Brilliant pebbles', the successor to the X-ray idea that proposed smart mini-missiles, which would be fired to collide with ICBMs and destroy them kinetically.

15 Victor Yeates, *Winged Victory* (London, 1961), p. 20. This biographical
    First World War novel, which deserves to be far better known, was described
    by T. E. Lawrence as 'admirable, wholly admirable, an imperishable
    treasure . . . one of the most distinguished histories of the war'.

SELECT BIBLIOGRAPHY

Bennett, Jim, and Stephen Johnston, *The Geometry of War, 1500–1750*,
    exh. cat., Museum of the History of Science, Oxford (Oxford, 1996)

Bridger, Sarah, *Scientists at War; the Ethics of Cold War Weapons Research*
    (Cambridge, MA, 2015)

Bud, Robert, Paul Greenhalgh, Frank James and Morag Shiach, eds, *Being
    Modern: The Cultural Impact of Science in the Early Twentieth Century*
    (London, 2018)

Calder, Jenni, *There Must Be a Lone Ranger: The Myth and Reality of the
    American West* (London, 1976)

Chivers, C. J., *The Gun: The AK-47 and the Evolution of War* (New York and
    London, 2010)

Churchill, Winston, *The World Crisis, 1911–1918* [1923–9], revd cdn, 2 vols
    (London, 1938)

Lord Fisher [Admiral Sir John Arbuthnot Fisher], *Memories* (London, 1919)

France, Catherine Ann, 'Gunnery and the Struggle for the New Science
    (1537–1687)', PhD thesis, University of Leeds, 2014

Gaddis, John Lewis, *The Cold War* (London, 2005)

Gibson, Langhorne, and Vice-Admiral J.E.T. Harper, *The Riddle of Jutland:
    An Authentic History* (London, 1934)

Gimpel, John, *The Medieval Machine: The Industrial Revolution of the Middle
    Ages* (London, 1992)

Goodchild, Peter, *Edward Teller: The Real Dr. Strangelove* (Cambridge, MA, 2004)

Hall, A. Rupert, *Ballistics in the Seventeenth Century* (Cambridge, 1952)

Hounshell, David A., *From the American System to Mass Production,
    1800–1932: The Development of Manufacturing Technology in the United States*
    (Baltimore, MD, 1984)

Hughes, Agatha C., and Thomas P. Hughes, *Systems, Experts, and Computers:
    The Systems Approach in Management and Engineering, World War II and
    After* (Cambridge, MA, 2000)

Husbands, Philip, Owen Holland and Michael Wheeler, eds, *The Mechanical
    Mind in History* (Cambridge, MA, 2008)

Lacey, Robert, *Ford: The Men and the Machine* (Boston, MA, 1986)

Latil, Pierre de, *Thinking by Machine: A Study of Cybernetics* [1953], trans. Y. M. Golla (London, 1956)

Massie, Robert K., *Dreadnought: Britain, Germany, and the Coming of the Great War* (New York, 1991)

Maxim, Hiram S., *My Life* (London, 1913)

Pemberton, William E., *Exit with Honor: The Life and Presidency of Ronald Reagan*, The Right Wing in America (Armonk, NY, 1997)

Pickering, Andrew, *The Cybernetic Brain: Sketches of Another Future* (Chicago, IL, 2010)

Pile, General Sir Frederick, *Ack-Ack: Britain's Defence against Air Attack in the Second World War* (London, 1949)

Scott, Admiral Sir Percy, *Fifty Years in the Royal Navy* (London, 1919)

Wiener, Norbert, *Cybernetics; or, Control and Communication in the Animal and the Machine* (Paris and Cambridge, MA, 1948)

Yeates, Victor, *Winged Victory* (London, 1934)

ACKNOWLEGEMENTS

It is a pleasure to thank Tim Boon, Head of Research and Public History at the Science Museum, for supporting this book, and the museum's director, Sir Ian Blatchford, for generously making the facilities and the collections of the museum available. Without this help the project would have been impossible. The Science Museum is special for a collegiate atmosphere and I thank friends and colleagues including Tilly Blyth, Robert Bud, Jim Bennett and David Rooney for many useful conversations and insights. John Roberts, friend and veteran bookman, helped to reassure me that it was not a foolhardy thing to attempt, when we discussed the germ of the idea so long ago. Adam and Chloe were invaluable in spurring me along to complete it. The faults and errors, of course, are my own.

PHOTO ACKNOWLEGEMENTS

The author and publishers wish to express their thanks to the below sources of illustrative material and/or permission to reproduce it. Some locations of artworks are also given below, in the interest of brevity:

Courtesy A. V. Hill Papers, Churchill Archives Centre, Churchill College, Cambridge, reproduced with permission of the Estate of A. V. Hill: p. 113; from The American Iron and Steel Association, *History of the Manufacture of Armor Plate for the United States Navy* (Philadelphia, PA, 1899), photo courtesy Library of Congress, Washington, DC: p. 82; from Horace Lucien Arnold and Fay Leone Faurote, *Ford Methods and the Ford Shops* (New York, 1919), photo courtesy Universiteits-bibliotheek, Vrije Universiteit Amsterdam: p. 56; British Library, London: p. 108; from Major Sir Gerald Burrard, *The Modern Shotgun*, vol. III (London, 1931): p. 100; photo Larry Burrows/The LIFE Picture Collection via Getty Images: p. 144; Burton Historical Collection, Detroit Public Library, MI: p. 170; photos California Historical Society, University of Southern California Libraries, Los Angeles, CA: p. 169; Carol M. Newman Library, Virginia Tech, Blacksburg, VA: p. 155; photo Howard Coster/Hulton Archive via Getty Images: p. 119; photo © David Penney Horological Picture Library, courtesy David Penney: p. 42; from Denis Diderot and Jean le Rond d'Alembert, *Recueil de planches, sur les sciences, les arts libéraux, et les arts méchaniques*, vol. IV (Paris, 1765), photo courtesy Smithsonian Libraries, Washington, DC: p. 34; photos © Ferrari s.p.a., reproduced with permission: pp. 73, 161; photo courtesy Fiat Chrysler Automobiles N.V., reproduced with permission: p. 63; from John Fisher, *Memories* (London, 1919), photo courtesy Robarts Library, University of Toronto: p. 79; photo James Fraser/Shutterstock: p. 166; photo Antonio Gallud (CC BY-SA 2.0): p. 61; The Henry Ford, Dearborn, MI: p. 55 (*foot*); Heritage Auctions, Ha.com: pp. 173, 188; photo © History of Science Museum, University of Oxford (Inv. Nr. 41591): p. 27; photo Chris Hondros/Getty Images: p. 206; Imperial War Museums, London: pp. 91, 94, 109, 110, 122; Lawrence Livermore National Laboratory, CA: p. 214; Library of Congress, Prints and Photographs Division, Washington, DC: pp. 168 (*top*), 171, 175; courtesy Malik Institute, reproduced with permission: p. 152; Massachusetts Institute of Technology

INDEX

Page numbers in *italics* refer to illustrations